MANUAL
LABOR

FEET AND SHOULDERS SQUARE, ELBOWS IN, EYES ON THE TARGET, FOLLOW THROUGH

DICK VAN SCYOC

We want to thank the Peoria Journal Star (Peoria, Illinois) and the Bloomington Pantagraph (Bloomington, Illinois) for allowing us the use of text for telling Coach Van Scyoc's story. We also want to thank the sports writers and photographers who so eloquently recapped local sporting events. You are amazing

FOREWORD

As the proud daughter and sister of the authors, Coach Dick Van Scyoc and Dr. Janice Bogle, it is with great pride, love and admiration that I encourage readers to indulge in a heartfelt personal story of the life of our father Coach Dick Van Scyoc. In this book, Dad and Jan painstakingly recreate the life of a young Van Scyoc. With interesting narrative and dialogue the two weave together Coach Van's professional journey and highlight historical events that shaped the man that would influence so many.

In an unpretentious application of facts and events, Jan seeks to uncover the relationships that are at the heart of the man that central Illinois came to know as *Coach Van*. Together, Jan and Coach Van have opened up a window into what made him tick. Jan was able to lead Coach into identifying what was important and what he wanted his players to learn. He revisited his coaching philosophy, his life lessons and as one player would term it, his *coachism's* that continue to influence exponentially. It would be his move, from a predominately white, rural farming community, to an inner city school on the south side of Peoria that finalized his own education; an education about people, relationships and loyalty.

His 45-year coaching career has touched many and we want to thank all the players, coaches and colleagues who have contributed in the telling of our dad's story. Through interviews, letters and artifacts Jan was able to assemble a narrative that engaged coach in his own story telling. We want to especially thank the Peoria Journal Star and the Bloomington Pantagraph. for allowing us to quote from former sports articles in telling dads story. We must also thank Bob Leavitt, Dick Lien, Mike Bailey, Fred Young and other sports reporters for their incredible writing. Without their diligence, creativity and interesting narrative in recapping on court play; this story could not have been told.

Gwen (Van Scyoc) Westendorf

TABLE OF CONTENTS

The Bridge Builder

Will Allen Dromgoole

An old man, going down a lone highway
Came, at the evening, cold and gray,
To a chasm, vast, and deep, and wide.
Through which was flowing a sullen tide.
The old man crossed in the twilight dim;
That swollen stream held no fear for him
But he turned, when safe on the other side.
And built a bridge to span the tide.
"Old man", said a fellow pilgrim, near,
"You are wasting strength with building here;
Your journey will end with the ending day;
You never again must pass this way;
You have crossed the chasm, deep and wide-
Why build you the bridge at the eventide?"
The builder lifted his old gray head:
"Good friend, the path I have come", he said,
"There followeth after me today
A youth, whose feet must pass this way.
This chasm, that has been naught to me,
To that fair-haired youth may a pitfall be.
He, too, must cross in the twilight dim;
Good friend, I am building the bridge for him".

CHAPTER 1
WHEN A FATHER PRAYS

He is happy who is active in accordance with complete virtue and is sufficiently equipped with eternal goods, not for some chance period but throughout a complete life.
Aristotle

NARRATOR:

Over the past few months when I visit my dad (Coach Van Scyoc), I am amazed at his zest for life, his ability to overcome adversity and his optimistic and encouraging attitude. He never feels sorry for himself, and he is always doing something to challenge his mind even at the age of ninety-four. In his early life he was a collegiate athlete, well known around Central Illinois. He graduated from Eureka High School in the spring of 1942 shortly after World War II was declared and he volunteered to serve his country. His story is not unlike that of so many other young men of his generation, planning a future after high school one minute and then being shipped overseas to fight in a war the next. He was fortunate to return from the European theater (England, France, Belgium and Germany) and enter college after three years away. His choices would impact many young men and women over his forty-six-year coaching and teaching career.

Coach has aged gracefully. He still rides his stationary bike, keeps his mind sharp with his iPad handy and reads novels the size of a small encyclopedia, ones that are often on the New York Times Best Seller list. If you need a good book to read, call and ask him to recommend one! Coach still travels from Illinois to Minnesota, a twelve-hour overnight trek to spend the summers at his beloved Daisy Island. This past summer when he and his wife Karen made the yearly trip, he maneuvered precarious obstacles: slippery docks, uneven landscape and a "big runabout boat". The boat ride completes the last two water-based miles of the trip. You can't drive to an island! Nothing seems to slow him down, and if you ask young men who have played for him, they will affirm his toughness and determination to get things done and done right. Some of their stories will be included in the following pages and will help explain what defines this interesting and endearing man. Much of the supplemental information contained under "Narrator" comes from me, Jan Bogle, Coach Van Scyoc's youngest daughter. I pull heavily from materials kept by Nettie Mae Van Scyoc, Coach Van's mother, my grandmother. She was meticulous and kept every newspaper article, letter or supplemental document about her son in scrapbooks. Mary, or Fuzz, as Coach referred to my mom, and Karen Van Waes, who would become my dad's second wife, would keep the scrapbook tradition going. But it all started with Nettie, as you can see from the letter that follows. The letter is printed in its original form without corrections.

Nettie, Dated April 2, 1946

Dear Son.

I knew you would be on the road until the 6th so I did not write. Dad and I are both ok. And hope you are to. We get the paper and also got your card. I am sure glad you got your first college ball for me – will you have it autographed for me. I am going to town tomorrow and get a new scrapbook as your old one is full and I want to keep all right ups. Mom.

As a character study, I have learned much about this man, my father, over the past years that this project has been unfolding. I have spent many days and sometimes weeks at a time revisiting the way and places of his life.

As an added bonus to finding out more about him, I have a written history that details eighty-one years of his playing and coaching days, through rich resources preserved by those who knew him best: Nettie, Mary and Karen. His words and actions speak highly of who he is. Lynn Collins, a Manual ball player on the '91 team, once told a Journal Star sportswriter that he wanted to be able to look Coach Van straight in the eyes when he met him on the street. He wanted to be able to say, "I did it right Coach", Lynn, along with many other ballplayers, would do it right; they took the opportunity afforded them by Coach Van and used it to their fullest advantage. Coach had the best interest of his players at heart, and it dictated what he taught them. If you ask Coach, he would say the real test, he believes, is whether a person can look him or herself in the mirror at the end of each day and feel confident they did what was right. Coach has a favorite poem that speaks to this very ethos. It's called *The Man in the Glass*.

The Man in the Glass

Peter Dale Wimbrow

When you get what you want in your struggle for self

And the world makes you king for a day,

Just go to the mirror and look at yourself,

And see what that man has to say.

For it isn't your father or mother or wife

Whose judgment upon you must pass.

The fellow whose verdict counts most in your life

Is the one staring back from the glass.

You may be like Jack Horner and chisel a plum

And think you're a wonderful guy.

But the man in the glass says you're only a bum

If you can't look him straight in the eye.

He's the fellow to please-never mind all the rest,

For he's with you clear to the end.

And you've passed your most dangerous, difficult test

If the man in the glass is your friend.

You may fool the whole world down the pathway of years

And get pats on the back as you pass.

But your final reward will be heartache and tears

If you've cheated the man in the glass.

Coach gave me access to all of his mementos, scrapbooks, yearbooks and other periodicals that told the story of his entire life, much of it playing ball. These artifacts provided a painted history with dates, times, places and people. The story started ninety-four years ago, a time when farming was the main industry in the country. It was a time when people were transitioning from horses to tractors and men would still sweat in the majority of jobs available across the country. The Ford Model T was hot off the assembly line. Smaller communities were still vibrant and optimistic about their future. Public schools provided local entertainment along with education, and school calendars were created around farm life. Coach Van grew up during this time, when kids walked from home to school and school to home. It was safe, and there was a deep connection between the community and the people. There was also value in this connectedness. Neighbors helped neighbors and lifetime friendships were forged, the kind that stood the test of time. So, the following pages will tell Coach Van's story in his words and from his perspective. There will be additional commentary from me the narrator, but the lessons are his.

COACH VAN:

Eureka, my hometown was a unique community. It was tucked away in the middle of Illinois farm country, and life was free and easy. Technology was a coal-fired furnace, a diesel fueled tractor and a Ford Model T, a step-up from a horse and buggy. We had an icebox and a telephone. When I used the phone I was likely to end up talking to a neighbor who was listening in on my conversation. It was called a party line. We were fortunate that my dad's job required a car, so we had an old Studebaker. Life was hard but good. I was taught from an early age that hard work breeds a sense of accomplishment. I was also taught that in our town people help each other.

That was the community I was born into, Richard Lee Van Scyoc on March 30, 1924. It was the decade of the "roaring twenties", flagpole sitters, speakeasies, prohibition and mobsters. Chicago was just two hours north of Eureka, Illinois, my hometown. Women had just won the right to vote. Racketeering was at an all-time high, and teachers could expect to earn around $960 a year while hoping to live to the ripe old age of fifty-four. Culturally, this was the time of George Gershwin's "Rhapsody in Blue" and crazy dances like the Charleston and Black Bottom Shimmy. Talking picture shows and movie stars like John Barrymore were the talk of the town. Another form of entertainment was growing in popularity, called The Ziegfeld's Follies. Mr. Ziegfeld was pushing the decency envelop by promoting Emil Jennings and Fanny Brice. The magician, Harry Houdini, was putting his life at risk to amaze people. Sports legends Roger Hornsby and Babe Ruth filled baseball stadiums full of people to show off what they could do with a bat and a little white baseball. This was the beginning of my life, and as I got older, I'd listen to my favorite team, the Chicago Cubs, on the Victrola. I listened to Bob Elson and Ronald Reagan as they described every play. I had baseball cards of each of my favorite players: Gabby Hartnett, Charlie Grimm, Billy Herman, Billy Jurges, Stan Hack, Kiki Cuyler, Frank Demaree and Charlie Root. It was that kind of fun that I lived for. But I digress.

I was born into a family of seven, including my parents Nettie Mae and John Van Scyoc. The closest to me in age was my sister, Mary; she was twelve years my senior. Next came my two brothers who still lived at home: Harold and Frank. Then there were Ethel and Harmol respectively, both married and out of the house, but Ethel lived just a few doors down the street. Mary had epilepsy, so this made it difficult for her to live at home. She stayed at the Dixon State School and Colony for Epileptics in Dixon, Illinois, about ninety minutes north of Eureka. It opened in 1919 and housed ninety-six patients. We would drive to Dixon to see her every two weeks or so, unless she was scheduled for a home visit. These were scheduled periodically to keep Mary connected to home and community.

Harold was the closest to me in age after Mary, and he became like my second dad, making sure I went to school, and had the baseball equipment I needed. He was twenty years my senior and encouraged me to play ball. Frank's interest was in music. Harold and Frank were the only siblings still living at home, and they weren't there very much. They both married and moved out when I was in elementary school. We didn't see Harmol much even though he lived in Eureka.

My dad, John, spent his days as a fireman for the Libby-McNeal canning factory in Eureka. As a fireman at the plant, he worked in the boiler room shoveling coal into furnaces. He worked six days a week and many Sundays. This was not an easy job, and when he came home from work, he was covered in soot. Dad got promoted to foreman, and this put him on twenty-four-hour call. I remember my dad working every day of the week. If he didn't go to the plant, he would be freelancing around the community, helping with construction or some other odd job to make a few extra bucks. When I got older, I helped out at the plant. I would work in the boiler room shoveling coal. It was a dirty job, and I didn't like it much. For Dad, it was steady work and decent money. My parents felt fortunate for that job and the income it generated because there were lots of people out of work. Eureka was better than most communities though because of the farm labor and canning factory.

Dad never complained about his lot in life and the hard work he endured. He did it with a sense of pride, and this taught me a lot. My only regret was the time I didn't get to spend with him. I was either playing ball or at school, and he was always at the plant or working. I'm not sure we would have hung out anyway; he wasn't into sports and he wouldn't let me help when he went on odd jobs. I think Harold told him to keep me focused on my pitching. They were hoping I would be the one Van Scyoc who would finish school, not just high school. They were pushing and preaching college.

Harold had enough baseball smarts to know I was good at pitching. As I got older, Dad encouraged me to practice and spend time playing with other boys in town. So, while Dad was helping build a house or lay a sidewalk, I was eyeing a batter and throwing a ball. Much of the time it was against the garage door in the backyard. I would use that door as home plate. I'd grip the ball in my left hand, turn it over a couple of times, with my eyes keenly on home plate to the left side of the bag. I'd lift my right leg high in the wind up, swing my arm and let 'er rip. I was always trying to catch a small corner of the plate. It felt natural and something I loved to do.

I often wish that my dad and I could have enjoyed baseball together. It was something I always missed. He wasn't home enough for us to get close. But I know we were luckier than most families during the depression. Many families were struggling to keep food on the table and stay together. We only knew a little financial hardship now and then, and I was grateful to my parents for that. Each week Dad would bring home $19 cash money, and Mom would keep in a tin jar in the kitchen. If he got extra money doing odd jobs, that went into the jar too.

Mom was responsible for making sure the bills got paid, because Dad didn't have much schooling. Mom did a lot of juggling during the winter when we would have about 150 to 200 pounds of coal delivered each month. We were often a little overdue on our payment, but we did get it paid. I was the one to deliver the envelope with the money, and I hated going to the lumberyard to make that one particular payment. The owner was condescending and he liked to call and harass Mom. He often made her cry. This really upset me and I often felt like setting him straight, but

I knew Mom would have been embarrassed and she would have given me the "what for" when I got home. So I kept my mouth shut and paid the bill.

Groceries were the only real necessity we had. During the summer months, Mom would harvest and can vegetables. This usually carried us through the winter. I didn't worry about clothes because I wore what every other boy my age wore: blue jeans, a t-shirt and a baseball cap. I was always outside playing ball when I was young. About my sophomore year in high school, I started wearing glasses. I worked in the movie theater in town and I think it messed up my eyes. I worked there to earn a little spending money and ended up spending it on glasses.

Mom was a stickler for cleanliness, and so I was always clean and presentable in my worn blue jeans and t-shirts. She would make a special trip to Montgomery Wards in Peoria to buy clothes for special occasions, nothing fancy, just new. We only bought things we needed. Harold used his paycheck to buy me a left-handed baseball glove, a bat and some baseballs. Harold played sports when he was younger but quit when he dropped out of school. He knew I liked playing ball and I was good, so he pushed me in that direction. Frank, on the other hand, played in the town orchestra and the Eureka College pep band. He didn't attend Eureka College, but back then you could play at the games in the pep band without being enrolled. Through my fourth to sixth grade, he would take me with him for the college basketball games.

We'd visit Mary at the state hospital every few weeks. Mom would make fried chicken, potato salad, baked beans and home baked pie, my favorite. Boy, could Mom cook! We would drive up in Dad's Studebaker. During the summers, we'd spend the afternoons on the grounds of the hospital, sitting on a blanket. Then after a few hours, we'd drive home. Mom hated leaving Mary. The trips were harder on Mom than Mary. Mary came to Eureka every couple of months and stayed a week or two, but always seemed to want to go back to her friends at the hospital. Mom wanted Mary to live at home, but her condition just wouldn't allow it. Mom would always get quiet on the ride home. Paying for Mary's care was a heavy burden on Dad and contributed to why he worked so hard. Mom and Dad did the best they could.

Eureka is a small community embedded in farm country, a very safe place where neighbors helped neighbors. We lived near downtown; the 100 block of Meyer Street, near a Texaco gas station, north of Highway 24. Our house was located a couple of blocks east from the bus stop and about a mile from the canning factory. Where I lived was considered "the other side of the tracks". We lived in an area of town that housed families who didn't have much. It wasn't a problem until a cute gal caught my eye in high school. Her name was Mary Kathryn Frerichs.

We didn't live far from the industrial and economic center of Eureka, including the business district. This area was the hub of local activity. The bus station, Michael's Sweet Shop, the Five & Dime were all located in this same area. Eureka had a small movie theater, a small hospital and a courthouse with a small amphitheater located on the courthouse lawn. The amphitheater was where my brother Frank's community band participated in patriotic events during the holidays. Local politicians made speeches, and people brought lawn chairs and blankets to listen to the music.

I have great memories from my days growing up in Eureka. I can remember the cool evening breezes, the fireflies we caught after dark and the fun we had watching them light up. The community would set off fireworks on the fourth of July, and people would put wreaths on graves at the local cemetery on Memorial Day. In the fall during Labor Day, people would conjugate on the courthouse lawn for picnics and band concerts. It was at this same time that farmers would line up in front of our house to bring their products to market. I would sit on my front porch and listen to the band play while watching the parade of tractors or horses pulling wagons full of corn or pumpkins to the local elevator to be weighed. Or sometimes I would be right inside the front door watching these same wagons and tractors, but with a less than honorable intent in mind. The farmers would line up for miles and would sometimes sit in front of our house waiting for the line to move. This became an interesting game for me because of Polly, our parrot. Polly joined our family one summer when we went to Nebraska to visit Mom's relatives. They wanted to get rid of the bird, so we took her. The parrot became our entertainment, well, the parrot and Dad. He hated that bird. He used to cuss at it, and it learned to cuss back. Boy, did it have a vocabulary that would burn your ears. When Dad was really mad, at the bird, he would take a glass of water and say, "I am going to throw water on you!" Then the bird would say, "Throw water, throw water", which Dad would do and then the bird would start squawking and telling anyone around to "Go to hell!" It was a sight to behold. We found out we could have a lot of fun when the bird was on the front porch. Some of those farmers heard that bird squawking and talking, but they couldn't figure out where it was coming from.

Mom and Dad didn't permit loafing. They were a good example of hard work and applying yourself to any task. Neither of my parents would cut corners. This was a lesson I learned early in life. I came home from school every day to eat lunch, but before I ate, I had to run Dad's lunch to him at the plant. After that, I would drop by my aunt's house with her lunch. Finally, I would hustle home and eat before returning to school. Things didn't always run smoothly at our house; during difficult times we just put our heads down and plowed through. But unfortunately, Dad's long work hours at the plant presented problems for him in his personal life. Sometimes he'd stop at the local tavern for a little enjoyment before coming home. Some of those nights I'd like to forget. Mom spent her time washing, ironing, hanging out clothes, cooking, cleaning house and paying bills. On top of these household chores, she made cakes for people around town to make a few extra bucks. And, of course, she took care of Mary when Mary came to visit.

NARRATOR:

John Van Scyoc, Dick's father, was a man who was aging prematurely under a heavy workload. His work was physically demanding. Mary's expenses at the state hospital had to be paid, and he was concerned for her health. He worked to invest in his youngest son who had come late in life but with an aptitude for schoolwork and baseball. John's own story was much different. He had little book learning. Now he understood the value of his son's gifts. To make sure Richard fulfilled his dreams, John sacrificed his time and relationship with his son. He pushed Richard to spend time playing ball with his teammates, as well as do homework and chores. John and Nettie began planting the idea that Richard would graduate from college. He heard this from both of them over and over in his young life. It was within this context that a typewritten poem, yellowed with age, corners crumpled, was found with Nettie's letters and mementos. It has been carefully safeguarded, and in it we see John and Nettie's hope for Richard.

When a Father Prays

(Author unknown)

Build me a son, oh Lord, who will be strong enough to know when he is weak and brave enough to face himself when he is afraid, one who will be proud and unbending in defeat:

A son whose wishbone will not be where his backbone should be; a son who will know, that to know himself, is the foundation stone of all true knowledge

Rear him, I pray, not in the path of ease and comfort, but under the stress and spur of difficulties and challenges. Here, let him learn to stand up in the storm. Here let him learn compassion for those who fall.

Build me a son whose heart will be clean, whose goal will be high, a son who will master himself, before he seeks to master other men. One who will learn to laugh; but never forget how to weep; one who will reach far into the future; yet, never forget the past.

And after all these are his, add I pray, enough of a sense of humor so that he may always be serious yet never take himself too seriously; a touch of humility, so that he may always remember the simplicity of true greatness; the open mind of true wisdom; the meekness of true strength.

Then, I, his father, will dare, in the sacred recesses of my own heart, to whisper: "I have not lived in vain".

COACH VAN:

I do not have many memories of Mary, my older sister. Her visits were a challenge for her as well as the family. Since she spent so much time at the hospital, it seemed as though it was where she preferred to be, even when visiting. Mary's epilepsy caused her to have unexpected seizures that could last over a period of hours, and the seizures interfered with her cognitive ability. This was a time when not much was known about epilepsy. Physically Mom did not have the strength to take care of Mary and Ethel would have to help. It was during the planning for such an upcoming visit that life took an unexpected turn. The winter holidays were approaching and Mary was coming to stay for a while.

Mom had gone to my sister Ethel's to make plans for the visit. It was after dark and it had been snowing. The streets and sidewalks were icy. While walking home Mom slipped and fell and broke her leg. She was hurting and in extreme pain. I'm not sure how she got home. Dad got the local doctor, Doc Nichols. He set Mom's leg at the house and told her to stay off of it and not do too much. That was easier said than done when talking to Mom. After a couple of days, Mom did what she could, hobbling around. Dad was concerned about her but didn't say too much. He knew Mary would require lots of care like daily grooming, food preparation and medication. Mom continued to look forward to Mary's visit. She thought she would be out of her cast by then. But before Mary arrived, Doc Nichols came back to check on Mom. Her leg was not healing and, in fact, had gotten worse. Doc had to reset the cast. This meant that he had to re-break mom's leg. I can remember that doctor visit vividly. I was upstairs in my room and I could hear Mom screaming. Doc broke her leg to reset it. It was something I had never experienced before. I had a hard time getting over what I heard knowing the pain Mom was in, I felt helpless. I know Doc had to do it, but I was terrified.

This was a terrible situation and I felt helpless, scared and sad. Mom and I had a real close relationship, a special bond. I became a mama's boy when I was young. I would tease her a lot, and I think she took special care of me because I was her baby. I would do a lot of chores around the house while Dad was gone, running errands and helping as much as I could. We spent a lot of time together, just her and me. Hearing Mom in that much pain had a profound effect on me. Doc Nichols ordered Mom to stay in bed, and this time she had no choice as he said she could potentially lose her leg. When Mary arrived, things got worse.

Ethel stayed at our house during Mary's visit, as Mom was bedridden. She couldn't do anything, and this made her miserable. She didn't like Ethel having to do all the work. It was during one of those long winter nights that Mary began to have problems. She just didn't seem right. The next day she had a seizure early in the morning. It didn't stop, so Doc Nichols was called again. By the time he got to the house, Mary had slipped into a coma. There was nothing anyone could do. He told us we would just have to wait and see. For the rest of the day and late into the night, Mary lay in bed. It was shortly before morning that she quietly passed away with Mom at her side. She died at age twenty-four. I remember these events well. I was supposed to play in a junior high school basketball tournament, but it had been cancelled because of a snowstorm. We had the wake and funeral at home. Mary was laid out in the dining room. Mom and Dad handled their grief with grace and dignity. With the help of friends and neighbors, we recovered.

NARRATOR:

Pastor Don Salmon conducted the funeral and sent a card after Mary's death. The card was received the day after Mary was laid to rest on January 1, 1938, and was lovingly kept with Nettie's scrapbook

Dear Friends:

This is a copy of the poem I used at the close of the service yesterday. I thought that you might want to keep it as a memorial.

Don M. Salmon, Pastor

She is Not Dead

"She is not dead, but sleepeth" the Master of men once said

Such words stirred the people for they believed her dead.

O Master of men and of ages, is death nought but a sleep?

Such a thought is priceless, buried in the heart so deep.

O glorious hope of the future, our dead are merely asleep

We'll not spend our days in sorrow; why should a Christian weep?

Sleep is followed by awakening; dawn's a new day for the soul,

God, heaven, and a new service, while eons of eternity roll.

Move on, O soul victorious, thy spiritual heritage keep

Hear these words of the Master, "She is not dead, but asleep".

Richard came along late in life for Nettie and John, the last of six children. Richard was twelve years younger than Mary. Then came Harold, Frank, Ethel and Harmol. It was quite a crew. However, only Frank and Harold were still at home for any length of time while Richard was young. Harold, eighteen years Richard's senior, would make a significant impact on his life.

COACH VAN:

Since Frank played in the town band, Mom thought I should give it a try. My brother was a good musician, so that meant that I would also be good at playing an instrument, right? Mom found a teacher, Mr. Malcolm, who drove from Peoria. I would walk to the high school for my saxophone lessons every week. The problem was that I had to walk near a small open field by the Texaco station down from our house. There was always a pick-up baseball game going on. So I would leave for practice, walk to the gas station, set my horn down behind the gas station door, pull out my baseball glove and go have a game or two. I would play for as long as I could and then still try to make it to my saxophone lesson. Needless to say, I would often be late and it was known by my fellow ballplayers that I might not make it at all. It all depended on how the game was going.

Mr. Malcolm was a no-nonsense kind of teacher, very strict. He got pretty fed up with me. I was ready for the same speech every lesson. Only, this one day he caught me off guard. I came running into practice out of breath with my horn in tow. My teacher had had enough. In a no- non-sense voice that said you had better listen and listen good, he pointed to the windows that lined the far wall of the room and in a booming voice said, "Richard go over there and throw that horn out the window!" Boy was I scared! Obviously that was my last lesson. Mr. Malcolm called Mom to tell her that he refused to "waste his time", as he put it. I did learn to play the Hawaiian guitar. It only took fifty-two lessons. I did this with my niece Velma and we both got pretty good. She was living with us at the time and was only a year older than me. The Hawaiian guitar was a fad and short lived. Music just wasn't my thing.

Frank and Harold were fun to have around while I was growing up. By the time I got to middle school, they were pretty busy with full time jobs and lives of their own. Frank played in the community band and worked at the local factory. Harold worked at Caterpillar in Peoria. They were about a year apart in age. Harold was someone I really looked up to. He had played sports although he did not excel. He left school early for a job and the money it would bring. He had a girl who lived in Washington, Illinois, and they were pretty serious. Harold was not stingy and always bought me things, especially sports gear like left-handed gloves and baseballs. He also was what you call a "looker". He was handsome and always wore the latest styles. When I knew he was getting ready to go out, I would lock myself in the bathroom and wouldn't let him in. He would have to slip a coin under the door to get me to unlock it. Harold was good-natured and took it in fun. He didn't think it was so funny when Frank teased him.

Harold had bought a new pair of spats, probably to impress Clara, his girl. In the 30s, men wore spats or short cloths that buttoned and sat above the shoe to cover the instep or ankle. They were all the rage for young people who wanted to look like the newest picture in the local Montgomery Ward's Catalogue. Frank was always needling Harold, and one night he got hold of Harold's spats and wouldn't give them back. They really got into it when Mom came in with her broom. She began hitting them with the broom telling them to get out of the house until they could behave. It was pretty funny. Harold and Frank didn't stay at home long; they both married. When they moved out, I missed all the fun we had.

When I was in elementary school, I spent quite a bit of time at that empty field down the street from us, always playing ball. I could play for hours at a time. No matter where I went in town, I had a glove and a catcher's mitt with me. I carried a baseball in my back pocket or the pocket of my glove. I could always find another kid looking for something to do. If there wasn't a game going on, I would play catch with any kid I could find. I would even supply the extra catcher's mitt if the kid didn't have one. One unusual catcher was my niece, Velma. She was a good ballplayer. Another relative I played with was my nephew Bob Van Scyoc. We played on the high school baseball team together. He was a few years younger than me and was a good catcher.

My next best choice for playing ball—if there wasn't a game to be had—was to play in the backyard. I would use the old garage as a catcher of sorts, with the balls banging off the side. I would also hit dead pears off our pear tree for batting practice. I could get into a pretty intense make-believe game all by myself. I would pitch to the side of the garage calling balls and strikes. I could do this for hours; pretending I was in the majors, eyeing the batter and throwing the winning pitch. Our garage still has dents in it; I checked it out a few years back when my youngest daughter Jan and I visited my old stomping ground. To my amazement, the house and garage were still there. The dents were still there too!

Growing up, I had a dog I called Spot. What boy doesn't, right? Spot was a small white terrier with a black spot covering one eye and ear. With both ears standing straight up, he looked just like the iconic RCA Victor dog used in the 1905 record ads. I don't know when Spot joined our family; but he and I were best friends, and when I was home, he never left my side. We went everywhere together. He had a high-pitched bark and used it when people came over. Whenever he heard a knock at the front door, he would fly across the hardwood floor and put on the brakes about midway between the kitchen and the living room. Then he would slide coming to a dead stop directly at the front door.

Spot was always with me when I was out back hitting and pitching balls against the garage. I often used pears for batting practice from our back yard tree. I did this when I got tired of pitching. I would walk back, collect a few pears and hit away. I would toss a pear into the air and whack it. It would explode and the pieces would fly into the yard. One particular day I threw a pear in the air. As I swung my bat back I hit something. I intuitively knew I hit Spot. I could hear it and feel it. I don't know how Spot got behind me but he did. Now he was lying on the ground and I thought he was dead. I was pretty young and this was my dog, my pal! What was I thinking, doing? I couldn't move. I just stared at Spot for a minute or two. Then I picked him up and carried him to my aunt Ginny's who lived behind us. What a crazy thing to do! With tears streaming down my face,

I ran and told Dad I had killed my dog and told him where I'd taken him. Dad held me for a minute and then got up to go check on my dog. I just lay on my bed and cried.

Dad found Spot on Aunt Ginny's back porch. He scooped him up and took him to the only veterinarian in town. His office was out by the college. To this day, I don't know how that little guy survived. Dad brought Spot home with some instructions to keep him quiet and resting for a while. When Spot was fully recovered, he looked a little different. One ear wouldn't stand straight up anymore. He didn't run quite as fast and he laid around a bit more, but he was no worse for wear. The one thing that did change was how I saw Dad. I never had close relationship with him because he worked so much and was never home. So I guess I equated that with him not caring. But he did care, and he cared a lot. He didn't have the time or the money to take care of that dog, yet he did. He never said anything to me about being irresponsible. He just helped my dog. There are other instances in which I got to see Dad's unbridled love for me and his deep concern for my well-being. It played out in different ways over the course of my life. One of those instances was when I wanted to play football.

CHAPTER 2
THE SOUTHPAW

Education is anything we do for the purpose of taking advantage of the experience of someone else. (Lyman Bryson, American Educator)

From a very early age, I remember hearing Mom and Dad say to me, "Lefty, you are going to college". There was no discussion, no explanation, just a matter of fact. I'm not sure I even knew what they meant – college. Mom just kept drilling it in that I would go to college. Dad supported her one hundred percent. None of my siblings finished junior high school, let alone high school. Now mom and dad were talking about me going to college. I was the youngest, and Mom was going to make darn sure her youngest son would end up with a college education.

School was what I did when I wasn't playing ball. I started attending Davenport Grade School in 1930. School started at 8:30 a.m. and I was always prompt. My first-grade teacher was Miss Workman, whom I vividly remember because I got to experience her ruler. She would whack my hand when I wrote left-handed. Being left-handed was how I got my nickname. Being a left-handed pitcher meant I was a southpaw, and so the name "Lefty" stuck. Mom would call me Dick or Richard. Being a left-handed pitcher had its advantages, but there was no advantage in doing anything else left-handed. It was during this time that schools used the *Palmer Writing Method*. We had penmanship practice every day. I would use my left hand and Miss Workman would correct me and make me use my right. It got to be a battle, and I was determined to win. My penmanship was going from bad to worse and I hated getting hit with that ruler. I started hating my teacher and school. Dad decided to step in. He went to school—which he had never done before—and told the teacher to let me write with my left hand. She gave me no more trouble.

Mrs. Roush was our principal and a truly fine teacher. She and I had many good talks when I attended Illinois Wesleyan College. She joined the Wesleyan faculty when I was a student there. One winter day outside of our apartment, I heard her yelling my name, "Richard, Richard". She had her arms wrapped around a small tree. She got caught because of the ice and couldn't get her footing. I couldn't believe it. I went out and helped her across the street to the administration building. It was lucky that I was home at the time. As a teacher, she had a great impact on me.

As a young boy I was fortunate to be blessed with size and some athletic ability. I was a three-sport athlete in high school. My athletic endeavors started very modestly as a basketball player on the junior high school team. I was good enough to get by in the classroom without studying hard. I excelled in what was important to me: baseball and basketball. When I entered high school, I added football as a sport. Playing ball was what I thought school was all about.

I entered Eureka High School in September of 1938, excited for the opportunity to play high school ball. We had a good crop of athletes. I was lucky that Dad and Harold gave me the opportunity to hone my skills well, and those early days of pitching to the garage were paying off. That garage took a lot of beating during those early days, but now I was in a position to pitch to real batters in real high school games. I played football, basketball and baseball during my four years at Eureka and earned twelve varsity letters.

Thanks to two teachers, Mr. Ed Major and Miss Helen Bone, I began to think that just maybe school was as important as playing ball. Mr. Major was my high school social studies teacher. He was tough and demanding, the kind of teacher that most kids hate. But he also was a teacher who garnered respect. Mr. Major was one of two teachers who had a big hand in keeping me headed in the right direction. He had the ability to motivate kids, get them to come to class prepared with their homework assignments completed; at least I felt a necessity to make sure I had my work done in his class. He continually stressed grades and college. Mr. Major was someone I respected, and his influence on me has lasted over the years. He was one reason I chose history as my field of study.

Miss Bone was my English teacher. She had a different method of motivating kids. She made an offer to me, and Frank Whitman, my buddy after sending us to the hall on more than one occasion. Her offer was in the way of a challenge. If we would buckle down and make the honor roll by the end of the grading period, she would take us to Purdue University for a visit on a Saturday and then to the Cubs baseball game on Sunday. I don't remember being too interested in visiting Purdue, but when she said Cubs baseball game, I was in! Frank still wasn't convinced and just shrugged it off. He said we could never do it. But this teacher had my attention. I talked Frank into giving it a shot. In fact, by the time I got done talking, I had Frank more convinced we could do it than I was. I had never made the honor roll in my life. I had just been too busy with important things like baseball. But at the end of the grading period, there it was: Frank Whitman and Dick Van Scyoc, Honor Roll! Wow! Even though the trip never materialized, my thinking change. I wasn't sure I was college material before, but now I had something on which to hang my hat! Miss Bone will never know what her challenge did for a kid like me, a kid who lacked confidence in the classroom.

It was while in elementary school that I worked my first job at the Texaco gas station. It allowed me a little spending money. I was responsible for setting out the oil and gas cans, sprinkling dry cement over grease spots and keeping the driveway clean. I also put out signs listing the different oil and gas prices. Mr. Ulrich was the owner who I promptly reported to at six thirty every morning before school. I also had to shovel coal in our furnace at home in the basement before leaving for work. I still remember those cold snowy days. I did what I could to help mom and dad before leaving for the gas station. I did this throughout seventh and eighth grade. I developed punctuality, responsibility and respect for authority that served me well. These were important skills for me to learn early in life.

NARRATOR:

When Richard wasn't working, he played ball. In fact, he played ball every spare minute he could find. His dad and brother Harold pushed him to play, and play he did. He got his start in American Legion Junior Ball and a newly instituted high school program. When Lefty was a freshman, there was no baseball program at Eureka High School. Parents convince the school board to add the sport. The school board was happy to oblige since they too saw the talent in these young boys. The local newspaper often misspelled Richard's last name, as you will see in the following article.

"BASEBALL COMES BACK TO EUREKA: Galbreath Will Coach High School Nine.

For the first time in almost a decade Eureka High School will have a base-ball team this spring. The sport was removed largely because of lack of an adequate diamond to play on. The interest was so strong this spring that the Board of Education agreed to place the great national game back on the school's spring sports program. While the new field is not yet equipped for baseball, it is adequate for practice. Home games will be played on the college diamond…. In the first game Friday at Roanoke Coach Galbreath plans to start 'Lefty' Van Syoc on the mound".

When American Legion Junior Ball began in Eureka, Lefty was a junior in high school. Some of Coach Van's fondest memories were playing Legion ball. Any young boy in the 30s and 40s who played organized sum-mer ball was most likely playing for an American Legion team. American

Legion Baseball, according to their current website (legion.org), explains the league as *"a national institution, having thrived through a world war, several national tragedies and times of great prosperity"*. The organization was founded in 1925 to help "war-weary World War I Veterans". It promoted sportsmanship, good health and active citizenship through its youth baseball organization. The American Legion baseball program is still going strong today and big league ballplayers talk fondly of their experience. Some of those players are Albert Pujols, Don Mattingly, Luis Gonzales, Yogi Berra, and Bob Feller.

Bob Feller (1936–41; 1945–56) was the first major leaguer who got his start in Legion Ball. The Cleveland Indians scouted and signed Feller at the young age of seventeen. Feller never played minor league ball. He went straight to the major leagues and after his career was over, was the first legion ball player inducted into the Major League Baseball Hall of Fame. He fondly tells of playing for The American Legion in Iowa where an umpire passed his name to the Cleveland organization. Feller believed in the importance of the league program, especially in developing rural youth. Coach Van's experience is similar, although he did not sign a major league contract.

COACH VAN:

During the summer of my junior year, I played ball for the American Legion Benjamin Haecker Post 466 with boys from Eureka, Roanoke and Washington. This was the first time the Eureka American Legion began sponsoring summer ball. We wore our individual high school uniforms, as the league did not have any money for gear. Different parents drove us to the games. It was a big deal in Eureka during the 1940's, as there was not much entertainment, and we ended up being pretty good.

A local Washington florist, Rex Martin, was our coach. His son shared pitching duties with me. Coach Martin had played baseball at Purdue and was known as a pretty good outfielder, in his own right. His son was a good pitcher. We had teammates like Frank Whitman, who would play for the White Sox, and John McEldowney, who was with the White Sox's farm team. Merle *Wuethrich* was with the Chicago Cubs farm team. Robert Newman, from Washington, IL, was 6'2" and a great athlete and baseball player. He would have made some major league team a heck of a player, but sadly he drowned at the end of our '41 season. It was a difficult time for all involved. He was swimming across Lake Eureka when it happened. It was a great loss to his family, his teammates and the community.

We had good ballplayers from around the area. During the school season, we played against our Legion teammates. Roanoke was one of those schools. Roanoke's Coach Cravens spoke fluent Italian since his parents had emigrated from Italy. He used this to confound teams Roanoke played against, communicating with his players in Italian. He would often eat at the local Eureka diner, Michael's Sweet Shop, just so he could tease us about it. Still, he was a good man.

We loved playing baseball, and the fact that we weren't a shabby team didn't hurt. We were good enough to upset Belleville and then beat Rockford to earn the right, as a central Illinois team, to play Chicago Berwyn, a powerhouse in Legion Ball. This was the first time any central Illinois team had made it to the downstate state playoffs, The official team roster included myself, Augie Martin (the Coach's son), Frank Whitman, Robert Newman, Bill Morrow, John McEldowney, Merle Wuethrich, and Jimmy Bussone.

NARRATOR:

Rockford and Eureka were the winners out of a slate of four teams (Rockford, Belleville, Kewanee and Eureka). The *Peoria Journal Star* newspaper reported that *"Rockford beat Kewanee a 'David and Goliath' battle while another southpaw, Dick Van Scyoc was the principal factor in Eureka's victory over Belleville"*. It went on to report: *"Van Scyoc retired fifteen straight batters"*. Eureka would have to battle Rockford to see who would go up against Chicago Berwyn, a baseball powerhouse who made multiple trips to the national finals. While the semi-final game was played in East Saint Louis, the *Peoria Journal Star* headlines told it all:

"EUREKA WINS DOWNSTATE AL BALL CROWN

A fighting American Legion baseball club that refused to surrender even in the face of erratic fielding came through with a seven run splurge in the sixth to defeat Rockford 9-6 here Sunday and win the downstate champion- ship. It is the first time in the history of the series that a Central Illinois team has ever won the honor. Out hit 9 to 8 and charged with six fielding mistakes, the Benjamin F. Haecker Post N. 466, bunched six blows in their big inning to crash the gates and take the championship back to Eureka (Martin pitching, Michelleti catching and Van Scyoc playing first base)".

Eureka had picked up quite a following of fans that attended the games. Lefty pitched against Belleville while Augie Martin pitched the next game against Rockford. Lefty happened to remember this tournament well, but the reason had nothing to do with winning. Lefty's dad John never attended his games, not in Eureka, not anywhere. But, this game was different. There was so much excitement in Eureka; the young Van Scyoc thought his dad might make the trip. Harold was planning on bringing their parents to see Lefty play, if John could get away. Unbeknownst to Lefty, Harold was plan- ning on making this trip. He would see Lefty pitch whether John came or not, and he was going to bring Nettie.

Lefty had been tapped to pitch against Belleville. As he headed to the mound, an announcement caught him off guard. The announcer let it be known that Nettie Van Scyoc, Lefty's mother, was in the stands seeing her son pitch for the first time ever. It would be quite a day. Harold and Nettie enjoyed seeing Eureka beat Belleville to advance in the tournament. Even though John wasn't there it was a swell day. According to Lefty, this was the only game either one of his parents ever saw him play.

The following Bloomington Pantagraph newspaper clippings highlight the sense of excitement and pride the community felt toward this group of boys and their accomplishments.

"Young's Yarns (by Fred Young)

The eyes of all Woodford County will be focused on East St. Louis this weekend where the annual downstate American Legion baseball tourney is scheduled for Saturday. Victory of the Eureka post in the fourth division here last week sent the pressure up to a high pitch in Woodford County and many legionnaires plan to accompany the members of the Benjamin F. Haecker post No 466 to East St. Louis. Coach Rex Martin has an outstanding ball club, which, if it is up to par in the series, has a chance to go places.

Martin has two fine young flingers in his son Aaron, a junior at Washington High School, and Dick (Lefty) Van Scyoc, a Eureka high school senior. Both boys are capable of making a fine showing at East St. Louis. Frank Whitman, Eureka High shortstop; Merle Wuethrich, second baseman from the same team, and Jimmy Bussone and John McEldowney, the two Roanoke boys, are all above average for their age. No boy who was 17 by Jan 1, 1941, is eligible for this series. The Eureka boys will meet stiff competition in the Belleville, Kewanee and Rockford winners but have the stuff to come through".

Following articles are about the Eureka/Berwyn three-game series played at Kankakee.

"Eureka Begins State Title Play Saturday: Woodford Boys Meet Berwyn at Kankakee.

The American Legion Junior Baseball championship will be decided next Saturday, Sunday and Monday at Kankakee . . . No games are scheduled this week until the playoff at Kankakee. It is Coach Martin's policy to rest his men before a tough series, as this is certain to be. Berwyn's baseball program is second to none in the state and Cicero (Berwyn) annually produces more outstanding young players than any other sector of Chicagoland.

The Eureka nine have a tremendous following in Woodford County and a large delegation of fans will accompany the Haecker Post nine to Kankakee Saturday for the series. Eureka has some splendid representatives on this club in Merle Wuethrich, second sacker; Frank Whitman, shortstop, and Dick Van Scyoc, talented southpaw . . ."

Van Scyoc pitched the first game in the three-game series against Chicago Berwyn, played at Kankakee.

<u>"Dick Van Scyoc Stars on Mound for Winners</u>

Dick Van Scyoc, pitching for Eureka behind uncertain infielding, turned in a beautiful job, allowing only seven well spaced hits, while big Joe Vydra (Chicago B), disheartened by his mates' fielding blunders, left the game when he couldn't retire the side in the ninth".

Joe Vydra was well known for his pitching prowess having played for a couple of years. He was considered a sure thing for the major leagues; it was just a matter of what team. Beating him was a great achievement for Lefty.

COACH VAN:

We ended up defeating Belleville in East Saint Louis for the downstate championship but lost to Chicago Berwyn in a three-game series (2–1). I remember that series like it was yesterday. I won the opening game defeating Berwyn 7–5. We came out swinging and scored two runs off of three hits in the first inning. Berwyn tied the score 2–2 in the second. Berwyn went ahead in the fourth by scoring twice. We scored single runs in the fourth, fifth, seventh and ninth to overcome Berwyn's lead and put Eureka in the winner's circle. Berwyn was a powerhouse and well known throughout the state for their junior league baseball success and the boys they developed that went on to play in the major leagues. I felt I had held my own with the best in the state and came out on top. This helped build my confidence.

Unfortunately, Augie Martin had a tough go with Berwyn in the second game. His dad dug in and left him in for the entire nine innings, using up any arm he would have left for game three. We were tied going into game three. I had pitched two days before and didn't have enough juice to get through the whole game with my best stuff. We couldn't call on Martin at all. We went down in the third game, but we gave it what we could.

I remember high school and Legion ball as some of the greatest times in my life. I pitched two no-hitters, the first against Chillicothe and the second against Woodruff High School. The Woodruff game resulted in no hits and no runs, pretty impressive for a school our size taking on a Peoria school and winning. In fact, we had beaten Central (6–5) and Woodruff (6–0) in state district tourney play. It is ironic that Peoria Manual High School knocked us out of contention, a school where I would spend twenty-six years coaching and teaching. The quality of players in our area brought out professional scouts and of course this made Fred Young's column in the Bloomington *Pantagraph*:

"*Bloomington Pantagraph -Legion:*

Eureka Nine Drubs Rankin, 10-2 in Legion Playoffs

Richard Van Scyoc, 16 year old Eureka high school athlete, twirled Benjamin F. Haecker post 466 to a victory over Rankin in the fourth division playoffs Monday at Normal in front of Nick Keller famous baseball scout and representative from Lake county".

My main focus was baseball while in high school. From 1937 to 1942, I had great mentors, role models and teachers including Mr. Spike Mason, the Legion supervisor, Reg Martin, my Legion coach, and Mr. C.C. Galbreath, my high school coach. I was impacted deeply by the devotion of these men to my development and those of my teammates. They helped me in many ways on and off the field. The influence of these men would be directly responsible for my first summer job as the American Legion

Program Director of Bloomington. But for now, when the weather didn't allow for baseball, I filled my time with football and basketball.

I started to play football without telling Mom and Dad. I don't know how Dad found out, but he did. I was on the football field listening to coach talk to us about the season, when to my dismay, I saw my dad heading our way. I could see him walking along the fence toward the field and coach. He didn't look happy. He had told me he didn't want me playing football as he thought I would ruin my chances for college and baseball. As he got closer, I spoke up to coach: "Uh, Coach, my dad is coming and he doesn't know I am playing football". Coach told us to take a lap. So all of the guys began running the length of the football field. I headed for the dressing room. I figured I would get dressed and skedaddle out of there without Dad being any the wiser. You would think I could figure he already knew I was there. It didn't take long before I realized I couldn't lie to Dad. I just never had, and I wasn't going to start now. It just wasn't something I could do. So I headed back out to the field.

Now I was feeling pretty grown-up and cocky. So when I met Dad on about the fifty-yard line, I told him I wasn't going to school if I couldn't play football. I knew the minute those words were out of my mouth; it was the wrong thing to say, especially to Dad. He shot back that he would drag me to school every day if he had to, and I knew he meant it. Then in a quieter tone and with no emotion, he said if playing football really meant that much to me then I should go ahead and play. Unfortunately, from that day on our relationship changed a bit. I can't quite put my finger on it, but I had hurt him. I don't know if he would have come to a game or two during the season, but now I would never find out. He never attended any of my games. I wish Dad had been there to see my eighty-five-yard return for Eureka's only touchdown against Farmington; Or my pass to George Chianakas for a touchdown that made its way into the papers: *Eureka touchdown in the 2nd quarter came from that reliable left arm of Van Scyoc who passed to Chianakas for a touchdown*". We had some great times, and I missed sharing them with my dad.

I had played basketball at Eureka High School for three years. We were pretty good, having great athletes, and on the *Eureka Prep Front* we kept rolling over opponents as headlines would indicate: *"Eureka High, Untamed in 14 starts, is Roanoke Foe at Metamora"* and *"As Woodford Cage Tourney Opens, Eureka scores 15th Straight Victory"*. Then I decided to sit out my senior year and concentrate on baseball. This was important news to those who followed high school sports. And in Eureka, that was just about everyone. People saw the high school teams as community entertainment. Our town took pride in the school and its athletics programs. But I had a laser focus on baseball and the opportunities it might hold. I had two no-hitters under my belt, Chillicothe and Woodruff. Woodruff was a school much bigger than Eureka and a baseball powerhouse. I had scouts watch me play, and this garnered some interest from pro teams. As bad as I wanted to play basketball, I stepped away because of eye problems and at the advice of my eye doctor. I was concerned about staying healthy for baseball and I believed the Eureka basketball team would do fine without me. Knowing there were barely enough players to make a team, the headlines read: *Green Hornet athletes to field a basketball team.*

Unfortunately, when the season-started Eureka's lack of a bench was evident and would cause problems late in the games. By then fatigued or fouls would begin to take their toll and Eureka wouldn't be able to finish strong. We were losing because of the lack of reserves. It was like the movie *Hoosiers*: we were a five-man team and we were struggling. Then, a bunch of parents and players came and asked me to join the team! Yeah, this really did happen. Of course, I had to say yes. I wasn't one to let my teammates down. Loyalty meant everything to me, and this would inform the way I approached coaching.

NARRATOR:

John and Nettie did not watch Lefty's ball games in person. Rather they followed his exploits through the newspaper articles that Nettie so carefully cut from the paper and pasted into the scrapbooks she kept for

Dick. John had limited schooling and reading was difficult. When John and Nettie were alone, they would sit down together and Nettie would read each article out loud so John could enjoy the success of his young son. They were his biggest fans. They left the decision with Lefty on whether he would play basketball his senior year. His decision not to play was explained in the Journal Star. *"The Green Hornets will also suffer from the loss of Dick Van Syoc who did not return for basketball this fall. Dick was the regular right forward for Eureka for three years"*. It wouldn't take long for Fred Young to update the story: (Again the *Pantagraph* would misspell Coach Van's last name.)

"January 16, 1942

Prep Pratter

By Fred Young, Sports Editor, The Bloomington Pantagraph

D. VAN SOYOC BOLSTERS EUREKA: GREEN HORNETS NOW HAVE FIRST CLASS RESERVE

 Everyone who took in the Pontiac Invitational early this month was sweet on this Eureka high school team. They seemed to have everything with the possible exception of reserves. It looked as if it were a five-man team. There was no first class reserve to call on when one of the boys got too aggressive. A tick, tack whistler could run this club shrewd observers agreed. Take the case of the Woodruff game. The Eureka Green Hornets owned a six-point lead with a minute to go. But they lost in the final minute of play.

 Now the situation has been relieved. A youngster named Dick Van Soyoc, who did some great hurling for Eureka's American Legion post nine here last summer, has joined the squad. Van Soyoc played regularly a year ago and was a good consistent performer. Above average, all agree. But his eyes were troubling him this winter and on his physician's advice, he did not go out for basketball. His eye condition has improved and now instead of five good boys to throw at the enemy, there are six. What a headache this team is for the other Prairie conference teams! And they are likely to go much further now that Van Soyoc has returned to the colors".

Fred Young, a sportswriter and an avid sports fan, would take Van under his wing. Their relationship would grow as Mr. Young would become a friend and mentor to the young Van Scyoc. One can only speculate that Mr. Young may have seen a bit of himself in Lefty. Young's greatest expectation, for the young left-hander, was that he would attend Illinois Wesleyan College, Young's alma mater; and then one day become a Sigma Chi. During Van's senior year in high school, Mr. Young had arranged for him to pitch batting practice to the Wesleyan Titans and stay at the Sigma Chi house overnight. Wesleyan was scheduled to go up against a left-handed pitcher in their upcoming contest with Milliken College. Van would provide the practice needed against a lefty. Events would not play out exactly as Mr. Young had imagined, but over time, Van would not let his mentor down. First there was a little business to take care of called a world war.

CHAPTER 3
CAMP HOWZE, TEXAS

Humility must always be the portion of any man who receives
acclaim earned in blood of his followers and sacrifices
of his friends. (General Dwight D. Eisenhower)

NARRATOR:

There are epochs of history when events are beyond our control; yet, there appears to be some sort of fate playing out. For the men and women of 1930s and '40s fate had a reckoning with history and for all, lives would forever be changed. This is the generation known as "the greatest generation" (1998, Brokaw, T.). Many would make the ultimate sacrifice. Tom Brokaw described this generation as "the greatest generation any society has ever produced" and argued theirs was not for selfish or immature benefits but rather they did what they had to because it was the "right thing to do".

COACH VAN:

December 7, 1941, Frank Whitman and myself along with our mothers were driving to Bloomington, Illinois, to have our senior pictures taken for the yearbook. We were listening to the Chicago Bears football game when the news broke in that the Japanese had attacked Pearl Harbor. Like others who heard the news, it was a moment I won't ever forget, but it was not something I fully comprehended at the time. As a community, Eureka citizens were aware of the political winds of approaching hostilities and had friendly arguments about America's role in foreign affairs. They had already been through one world war. But as high school students, our focus didn't go much further than the Friday night game and who was leading in the conference. For us, it was all about ball games, dating and what we were planning on doing after high school. Our worries, if we had any, were local. In any case, the local paper let us know that the long reach of war was being felt in and around Eureka. The names of boys drafted and required to report for service were already being listed in the local paper.

The following morning the teachers hustled us into the auditorium where we heard the broadcast by President Roosevelt declaring war on Japan. Little did we know what those words meant for our futures? For now, I continued to play ball, go to school, get my grades and think about the big leagues. Within one week of getting my diploma (May of 1942), I was on my way to Danville, Virginia, having been contacted by Elmer Yoter, manager of the Boston Red Sox's farm team in the Bi State League. I felt I had an opportunity staring me in the face. Frank Whitman had joined another Boston Red Sox's farm team in the Piedmont League, but was going to be joining the Danville team in due time. He would eventually play major league ball along with some of my other teammates. We were a pretty impressive group, and the newspapers wrote of our fortune.

Fred Young had been following my career and I was happy to have his advice. Of course, Mr. Young pushed college, along with my folks. But when Danville contacted me to come and play for them, I couldn't resist. I was there for about a month and was scheduled to pitch the next day when I received a telegram from Mr. Young. Mr. Yoter, the manager, wasn't real happy when he handed it to me. Mr. Young knew if I pitched in a league game, I would forfeit my amateur status and ruin any chances of getting an education while playing college ball. He made his feelings clear in the telegram, and because of my respect for him, I packed up what little belongings I had with me and hitchhiked home, a kid who had never been out of Eureka. I didn't have a dime to my name when I left Virginia and I am not sure how I made it all the way to Eureka. Mr. Young, along with my parents, was determined to see me in college, Illinois Wesleyan University to be exact.

NARRATOR:

Coach was a good athlete, a left-handed pitcher with opportunities opening in his favor. He also had forged a relationship with a sports columnist in Bloomington, Mr. Fred Young. Mr. Young became a *guardian angel* to the developing young southpaw. Nettie and John wanted Dick to go to college and so they preached that message every time they got a chance. Mr. Young had attended Illinois Wesleyan College and brought a unique perspective, a lived experience that was important for this young athlete to hear. This was a time when high school kids considered many different career paths once they left high school, an accomplishment in itself. Not everyone went to college or even thought of college as important. High school graduation was the pinnacle of success and meant getting a decent job, working in a factory or on a farm or going into trade. Most parents saw it as a time for their children to start earning a living.

Mr. Young had a strong relationship with lots of the boys on the baseball diamond. He was a sportswriter who typed one finger at a time. He was well respected in the central Illinois communities he wrote about, visited and embraced. He also was very well connected throughout the state and inside the halls of congress. Mr. Young did not wait to give Van time to sign a contract. He contacted Nettie and John immediately and told them not to sign anything as Van was only eighteen, while at the same time he sent the following compelling telegram to Van in care of Yoter, the club manager.

<u>Western Union Telegram</u> - <u>June 6 (1942)</u>

<u>To Richard Van Scyoc care of Danville VA baseball club</u>

"YOU WILL BE MAKING ONE OF MOST SERIOUS MISTAKES OF YOUR LIFE IF YOU SIGN NOW FOR IF YOU DO YOU WILL BE KICKED AROUND FOR FIVE OR SIX YEARS AT HUNDRED DOLLARS PER MONTH. I CAN MAKE MUCH BETTER DEAL FOR YOU IF YOU WILL SEE ME. DON'T SIGN UNDER ANY CIRCUMSTANCES AND SOME DAY YOU WILL THANK ME FROM BOTTOM OF YOUR HEART. I KNOW" FRED YOUNG

This was a turning point in Van's career. Even though he had promised Mr. Young he would be a Wesleyan Titan, he enrolled at Illinois State Normal College (currently Illinois State University), located in Normal, Illinois. This was one; of a very few *normal* teachers' colleges in the United States, specifically chartered to train teachers. It was located close to Wesleyan's Campus. Lefty's enrollment at Illinois State Normal came as a huge shock and disappointment to Mr. Young. Van let Mr. Young know that it would be a short-lived experience as he had already enlisted for the service and would be leaving in January. He only enrolled at Normal to play ball with some former teammates. He promised Mr. Young that he would enroll at Wesleyan on his return. Van took his first step in what would become his chosen vocation: teaching and coaching.

COACH VAN:

When I returned to Eureka from Danville, I enrolled at Illinois State Normal College. This was before I could let Mr. Young know that it would only be for a semester and that I would enroll at Wesleyan as soon as I returned from the service. To my surprise, I received a fiery card from him. He expressed "shock" and wrote, "I can't take no for an answer". Young reiterated that I was "too good of a pal to let him down". He ended the card with, "there must be some way we can work this out". The card was signed "Sincerely, Fred Young" and received on August 31, 1942.

My decision to enroll at Illinois State Normal College was never intended to hurt or betray my good friend. It actually was based on just wanting to play some ball with boys I knew from junior league play. For me, it was just a matter of time before I would leave for the service and I saw Illinois State as a kind of diversion until then. I relayed this to Mr. Young and committed to Wesleyan upon my return from the service, God willing.

I tried to enlist with the US Marine Corps and when they turned me down I tried the Air Corps. Neither would have me because of my eyesight, so I joined Uncle Sam's Army! My future was being dictated by events beyond my control. These were tumultuous times. Young men in the area were headed to different bases throughout the United States, serving in different branches of the service. My friends and fellow students were scattered throughout the country serving in the navy, air corps and army. We would eventually be shipped to different theaters throughout Europe and the South China Sea. When I stepped on to the bus for Saint Louis I was nervous and a little frightened. I had no idea where I would eventually end up. Was it possible that I would never see Eureka again?

NARRATOR:

It was Mr. Young's letters and his dedication to the boys from the Eureka area serving overseas that would define loyalty and unknowingly influence Coach to live by a similar code in his own life. Letters that Mr. Young wrote became a lifeline to those lucky enough to receive them and provided a window to home. When Coach left Eureka, he ended up in Fort Howze, Texas. His first assignment was with a bakery company and, from the sounds of it, not something he was that fond of. It definitely wasn't anything like his mom's cooking. Coach had tried out and was tapped for the baseball team. He would soon be heading to California and special services to play ball for the troops, helping with their morale. Many boys wrote letters to the *Journal Star* and a few were published, including Lefty's.

May 2, 1943

Dear Editor and Friends:

A few lines to let you know I have been receiving the Journal each week and read it from cover to cover. I appreciate the Journal very much and I will be looking forward to it in the future as I have in the past.

I have enjoyed the army very much the last month. The first couple of months were all right, but I didn't like the idea of being a baker. I guess the army decided I wasn't a baker also, and I am now a clerk in the office. I take care of the sick book, moving report, rations, and duty roster. I enjoy this work very much.

I will have to admit I don't like Texas. I am still looking for my first steer (cow). I expected to see a great many of them, and as yet I haven't even spied a cowboy. I don't expect to be in Texas much longer, and I am hoping to see California next.

I would like to say hello to all my friends in the service and wishing them all the luck in the world.

I would be happy to receive letters from any of my friends, and promise to answer them all. Thanks again for the Journal, and keep it coming. Sincerely, "Lefty". PVT. R.L. Van Scyoc, 262nd Q.M. Bakery Co. Camp Howze, Texas.

Nettie included a poem cut from the paper and pasted it below Lefty's letter telling about his first couple of months in the bakery company. Could it have been written at the same time? We can only speculate.

"Eggy Ode (author unknown)

The ETO is now my home,
And so I write this little [poem]
In honor of a dish that we
Are fed each morn at reveille.

Those golden-yellow powdered eggs

(The one for which the soldier begs)

Are oft the target of much hate

When they are heaped upon our plate.

My mess-kit shudders when the cook,

To whom we give a dirty look,

Reaches in his GI pot

And comes up with a mess of rot

That looks like eggs, the kind we know-

But, sad to say, it isn't so,

"It's good for you". The cooks all cry

"Just eat 'em up, and by and by

you'll be the soldier we adore.

A tribute to the Signal Corps".

You cannot get away, you see-

They haunt the menu constantly.

Oh save me from these powdered eggs

The kind for which the soldier begs!

O Comrades, do you really know

The thing that helped us strike the blow

That swept the Nazi from his legs?

Those nauseating powdered eggs!"

The paper also reported Lefty's first furlough, an unusual turn of events that he talks about in the following segment.

"Corp Richard Van Scyoc Eureka was home only one day on a furlough until orders came from Uncle Sam to report back to Camp Howze, Tex.,

indicating that the little portsider, who attended Normal this year, is headed to a new port".

COACH VAN:

Even though I didn't find the army that bad, I missed the folks and my girl, Fuzz. I missed the Eureka community and the familiar sights, sounds and smells. After being at Fort Howze for a few months, I was lucky and earned a pass home. I couldn't wait to surprise Mom and Dad. I hadn't told the folks I was coming. I rolled into town on the bus at about midnight one snowy evening. When I departed and started walking home, I was shocked to see the silhouette of my parents huddled together walking toward me. They had received a telegram early in the morning from the army informing me to return to camp immediately. My unit had been put on alert. That's how they found out I would be on one of those buses. Mom and Dad spent their day walking to the bus station to greet every bus that arrived starting early in the morning. I was on the last one. I spent the night at home and then headed back first thing the next morning. It was tough saying goodbye.

While at Fort Howze I tried out for the base baseball team. I was quite surprised to find out that I made it and was going to be playing baseball with special services. I was transferred to San Bernardino, California Camp Danby, with the 691st Quartermaster Laundry Battalion. For my new assignment, I played baseball. There were multiple bases in the vicinity and a huge number of troops waiting for orders. We played ball to keep the morale of the troops up and to keep them occupied when they had down time while waiting for deployment.

I also drove the basketball team to other camps for games. The sweet part of this assignment was I was doing what I loved and I got to see Mom and Dad every night. They had moved to Riverside, California, just fifteen minutes from where I was stationed. I got to eat and sleep at home. This came about when Mom and Dad decided to visit mom's brother who lived in Eureka, California, not too far from where I was stationed. On their way, they stopped to visit me and ended up staying, I mean actually staying and moving into an apartment in Riverside. Dad got a job as a plumber's apprentice. This is where they eventually built a small home. This was their permanent residence until they passed away. While stationed at San Bernardino, I could come home at night and then return to base in the mornings. Sometimes I was lucky enough to score a jeep. I would drive myself home, spend the night and hightail it back to base early in the morning. If I couldn't get a ride, Dad would swing by and pick me up and then take me back early.

I was fortunate to be playing ball and savored the assignment. It was just a matter of time before I shipped out. Like everyone else, my orders came. I told Dad on the way home that I had received orders and would be shipping out the next day. I wouldn't be coming home anymore. He waited until after I left the next day to break the news to Mom. I just couldn't say goodbye to her. As I boarded the troop train with the other soldiers, I couldn't help thinking about Mom and Dad and if they would be okay. Here they were, in California, away from friends and family. For a brief moment I worried about how they would make out if I didn't get back.

I was now bound for New York and a ship transport. What lay ahead, I did not know? We traveled from California, through Illinois and of all things made a stop in Bloomington! I couldn't believe it. My girl was just thirty-five minutes from the train station, but we were not allowed to contact anyone. So I asked a Red Cross volunteer to call Fuzz and tell her I had been close to her the day before. My journey was just beginning.

NARRATOR:

As Mr. Young watched the early days of Van's athletic career take shape, he saw the talent of a competent left-hander. He would watch the southpaw finger the ball, eye the batter and with a high kick deliver the pitch right across the corner of the plate. Not only did Mr. Young see a competent athlete, he saw an individual that took responsibility seriously and was kind and caring to those around him. It was the way he carried himself, his dedication to those he loved and a desire to always get better, be better at what he did. This was how he approached life. Over time, a strong bond developed between the two men.

Mr. Young's letters, carefully catalogued by Nettie, appear to knit time together. The letters that traveled to and from the battle-torn countries of Europe took months to arrive, but for the boys overseas, they provided a window to home. Dick looked forward to these letters and couldn't wait to read each word. Nettie fondly protected this rare peek into history by putting each letter into its own plastic protective cover. They grace one whole scrapbook and give a picture of Van's journey overseas. Short excerpts are included below. They begin:

May 6, 1942: *We are all hoping you will see fit to come to Wesleyan for your college work.* Fred Young

February 23, 1943 *Dick, Your letter of last night came as a welcome surprise . . .. I have in mind a series of stories from boys in the service on what they think of continuing baseball at home and if you will do so. I would appreciate a letter from you on this subject. Do you think we should go in other words? Write me very frankly if you don't agree . . .. Do write often. Fred Young*

These opinions represent answers from Bloomington-Normal boys in seventeen different states throughout the union and many from foreign lands and in all branches of the service.

Dean Buckles (Alaska), seaman second class- "I think all sports should be continued at home. The boys in the service like the games and listen to them over the radio. It helps the boys forget about their troubles and most of the boys get their home newspapers and follow their own high school and college teams religiously. It's a great builder of morale".

PVT R.L. Van Scyoc (Texas) urges that all schools continue their sports programs. He also adds that the Municipal league here can serve a real service

this year if the older men, who are married and needed at home will help coach the boys under 18. The newspapers are watched like hawks by the boys and are a big boost to morale in our camp- by all means carry-on.

Finally, Col. Gerald C. Thomas (26-year vet) says "as to overseas, probably news of one day's game on Guadalcanal provided more interest, more rec- reation more diversion, and a better tie with the homeland than could be accomplished by the arrival of a ship's load of morale specialists". It was found to be overwhelming. Continue sports at all levels in anyway possible.

<u>July 7, 1943</u> *Had a nice letter from Frank Whitman this week . . . Call on me anytime. I can do anything for you. Everything I have is at your com- mand.* Fred

<u>September 8, 1943</u> *It is grand to hear from you . . .. Now that Italy is out of the picture, I believe we will go after Germany hammer and tongs and once we get Herr Hitler in his place, I have a notion that the Japs won't be too tough so I am not one of those who thinks this is going on for five or six years. The sooner it comes the better, Dick, for everyone.* Fred

<u>June 7, 1944</u> *Dear Dick, A lot of water has passed over the dam but I want you to know that I am just as interested in you as I was when you were in high school and I am hoping that you will keep your word this time and make a fresh start at Illinois Wesleyan, when the peace comes, which I believe is in sight now. I can't believe those Kraut Eaters can hang in there much longer with all that bombing and that great army they have over there now. One of my best friends in the Senate says five million men overseas now… Hope you are twisting that old No.2 around them this year, and do write me some day. With every good wish, I am yours very sincerely, Fred.*

<u>October 25, 1944</u> *There is no one I would rather hear from than you so you can be sure that your letter was very welcome. Our 'pore little 17 year olds and 4-Fefers are doing all right . . . and will be ready if they are called. Personally, I hope they are never called and somehow or other, I feel like*

spring, we will be getting back to normal. I am praying for as much for you and my other friends in the service.

April 9, 1945 I am only praying that you are safe and sound. The news is good and I am hoping by this time next year you can be winding that southpaw hook around some of these Ivy League batters eyes. I have every reason to believe as much on what comes to me from the south Pacific and Germany. Frank Whitman and his pal Johnny Gabos who is coming with him to Wesleyan write me often and they are optimistic…and if my prayers are answered I know you are coming back whole. P.S. Don't ever fail to call on me if there is anything you need –money or otherwise and I will have it to you posthaste.

May 5, 1945 Your letter of April 26 reached me today and I hasten to reply because I want you to know how happy I am that you are at least safe up to date and I am hoping that the worst is over in the sector at least. In fact, after Germany is completely eliminated I can't help but feel that we shall make short work of those friends in Japan…You'll be with a great gang here after the war Dick and I can't wait to see you. Since your college was interrupted you should be one of the first to get out when the peace comes which it is bound to do. In the last war, they let those out with dependents first and then those with college ahead of them who had withdrawn to enter war. That should put you in front and by fall at least. We'll be praying for you, Fred.

October 24, 1945 I am glad to learn you are on your way out, and the good news can't come too soon for me either. I have a notion it may be sooner than you anticipate now. They tell me in Washington that they are getting tremendous pressure, and every effort will be along that line between now and Xmas. Frank is in a deployment camp in France . . . Health and Happiness always. Fred.

Nettie added another clipping, but this had little to do with Fred Young:

Peoria Journal -Sunday May 2, 1943: *"Mary Kathryn 'Fuzz' Frerichs is wearing a diamond. The lucky fellow is Sgt. Richard 'Lefty' Van Scyoc in the armed forces overseas. Fuzz is the Eureka Plant office timekeeper".*

COACH VAN:

I started pitching at Fort Howze in Texas and then in California. Back home, the local paper kept tabs on what I was doing, with tidbits like the following: *"Dick Van Scyoc, the Eureka youth who attended State Normal a year ago is now pitching for the Army baseball team at the desert training center near Los Angeles, California and is giving a fine account of himself".*

When I was shipped overseas, I continued to have opportunities to pitch and I loved these times. It took my mind off of the war and brought me a little closer to home. My talent for playing ball got me out of infantry drills. I would much rather handle a baseball than a gun. We always had a friendly game going and it got around who could really play. I remember a softball game in France against a well-known unit from back home, a black unit. The units were segregated by race during the war, which didn't make much sense seeing that we were fighting for freedom against a Nazi ideology that believed one race was better than all the rest. These black soldiers were just as committed to the United States as any of our white units, and they were also excellent baseball. As a baseball team, this unit was really good. We weren't bad either, and we thought we had a secret weapon: a professional pitcher.

Money started flowing as guys began betting on the game. I played first base. During the seventh inning, tempers were starting to heat up and I was hoping the game would end without any punches being thrown. These guys had been gone from home way too long and tensions were high. The game was tied, and now things were really scorched as I was on third base and in scoring position, ninety feet from home plate. I had some harebrained idea I could steal home. We would win, end of game, right? When the pitcher let go of the pitch, I took off down the third base line. Here came the throw, right on target. I heard "Your Out!" and that was it. Game over. I had a little egg on my face as I had to face my teammates. The game ended in a tie, which was probably not a bad thing. It cooled everybody off and the sergeant had to hand all of the money back. I was just glad to get out of there with my skin! What a game.

My experiences slogging across France, Belgium and Germany were not that extraordinary other than I saw the futility of war. The utter destruction was more than I could comprehend. I sent Fuzz a postcard that expresses this sentiment.

Sgt. R.L. Van Scyoc 36444022

47th Med. Dep. Co.

APO#408, c/0 PM

New York, NY

Mar. 19/45

Hi Honey:

Picked up a couple of cards while I was in Rouen (France), and I am sending them to you. Rouen was one of the four largest cities in France before the war but I don't know about now. There is not much left and you can guess why. Want to write you a letter now so better get busy. All my love, Lefty

I said a prayer that our country would never know the destruction on the scale and to the extent that I witnessed at nineteen years old. We soldiers did find ways to amuse ourselves and keep our minds engaged. Often, we would follow sports from home and test our knowledge by quizzing each other. Nothing was off limits: boxing, baseball, football, and hockey. We also played cards. I read the newspapers we received from cover to cover and tried to keep up with the local sports teams. I often wrote to Mr. Young, and some of my letters made it into the Bloomington *Pantagraph*— *Young's Yarns:*

I am writing to you to settle an argument that arose in a ball game Saturday. One was out and bases loaded. The batter hit one to the third baseman who tagged third base, forcing the man coming up from second. The man on third did not run for home but the third baseman threw the ball home anyway. The argument is: Is the runner who stayed on the bag safe or out? I say he is safe. The boys who said he is out are mostly from Brooklyn, and I, being from Illinois would like to know who knows most about baseball. Pfc. R. Van Scyoc, Camp Howze, Tex.

Mr. Young answered me in his column:

You win by a knockout. The man on third is entitled to the bag to have and to hold. Wonder why the third baseman did not throw to first for a double play and retire the sides.

As the war in Europe appeared to wind down, we were put on a transport ship filled with troops headed to the Philippines. I had been in France, Belgium and Germany. Hitler had fallen, and now we were on the move, headed to the Japanese Theater. I don't know how long we were at sea. I remember hearing the loudspeaker: "*NOW HEAR THIS! NOW HEAR THIS! JAPAN HAS JUST SURRENDERED. THE DESTINATION OF THIS SHIP IS NOW UNKNOWN*". It was August 15, 1945. Men let out cheers and went wild. I saw every emotion you can imagine. Lots of boys broke down out of sheer exhaustion, relief and joy. The next day we heard the speakers again: "*NOW HEAR THIS! NOW HEAR THIS! THE DESTINATION OF THIS SHIP IS NEW YORK HARBOR*". It was surreal. We couldn't believe it. I went downstairs to my cot and lay down and cried. I was going to make it home. There was laughter, tears, exhilaration and joy! Those sailors shot every big gun they had until they were out of ammo. If an attack came, we would have had to resort to spit wads to defend ourselves. And of course, my fellow soldiers began an early celebration drinking whatever they could get their hands on until they passed out. I was too relieved to ruin it, and I never had been a big drinker, probably from seeing it around home. So I didn't drink one drop. I just watched. It was pandemonium. It was hard to believe the war was over and we were going home.

Sailing into Boston Harbor was a moment in time that was surreal. I never thought I would see home again when first stepping onto a transport ship three and a half years earlier. Now, I was on another one that was jam-packed. We were a strong troop of over five thousand soldiers covering every deck imaginable to get our first glimpse of the grand ole US of A. Cheers, hoots and hollers broke to the sky, and I can attest that there wasn't a dry eye on that ship. Boston had an embarkation center, our first stop before being sent to Camp Grant in Rockford, Illinois. I was finally going home.

When we arrived at Camp Grant; described as a separation center, we found out it had previously been a medical training facility and was also used to house prisoners of war. It was a sprawling camp with some permanent buildings and also lots of tents. We called it tent city, where thousands of troops stayed before returning home. Release was granted on a point system. You earned points for being in a war zone, length of time you served, different branches and different places served. I was lucky being so close to home. I got to go home to Eureka on weekends and would bunk with my brother Frank or Harold in Washington since Mom and Dad still resided in Riverside, California. Fuzz would pick me up on a Friday and take me back on Sunday. I was there for a couple of months waiting on my discharge. It came January 19, 1946, and was official on the twenty-second.

A day before I was to be discharged and leave camp for Eureka, I was walking back to my barracks. I couldn't believe my eyes when standing in front of me was Frank Whitman: classmate, teammate and good friend from Eureka. He was as surprised as I was, and it was amazing that we even ran into each other. The place was like a small city with thousands of troops. If we knew we were both there, we couldn't have found each other if we had tried. It was a great feeling to see someone from home. We gave each other a big hug, and then we couldn't stop talking. Frank was waiting for his discharge just like me. His came one hour before mine. You just can't make this stuff up. Fuzz picked us up at the same time and that was it. I was no longer part of Uncle Sam's Army.

I bunked at Whitman's house until I could find my own accommodations. His parents didn't mind at all. It wasn't long before Mr. Young got me a job at the Soldiers' and Sailors' Children's Home in Bloomington. The job came with free room and board. I was granted release from the army on Tuesday; January 22, 1946, and I was attending classes at Illinois Wesleyan University on Monday morning; January 28, 1946.

CHAPTER 4
THE WESLEYAN TITANS

They can conquer who think they can.
(Quote next to Richard "Lefty" Van Scyoc's picture– The
Senior Nautilus, High School Year Book, 1942)

NARRATOR:

Coach Van was discharged from the service on January 22, 1946, and was enrolled and attending classes at Illinois Wesleyan College on January 28 that same year. This was a time when many young returning service members were enrolling in college in record numbers, compliments of Uncle Sam and the GI Bill. It had been three long years, almost to the day, when Lefty had stepped on a bus headed for Saint Louis and parts unknown. Now, he lived with his friend and teammate, Frank Whitman. It would be just a short time before Fred Young would find a job for Lefty at the Illinois Soldiers' and Sailors' Children's School, ISSCS. Lefty would live at the Sigma Chi house after pledging, fulfilling a promise to his mentor Fred Young. Frank Whitman would also pledge; but quit before becoming a Sigma Chi, not being able to put up with the juvenile antics of college boys who had not tasted the likes of war. Lefty was fulfilling a promise to Fred Young. Lefty would play summer ball for ISSCS in the Bloomington Municipal League, a "Double A" league, and college ball for the Illinois Wesleyan Titans. It was the local paper that kept the community in the know. Reporters wrote that *"Van Scyoc Mastered Redbirds at Every Stage 12-2"*, and that he would *"Blank Elmhurst with 5 hits helping Wesleyan win its third straight shutout, 7-0"*. The paper would report that Wesleyan would *"Pelt Murray State 13-2"* with Lefty and McDonald *"Sharing Laurels"*. It would report that in a second game with their biggest rival, Lefty would *"beat Illinois State Normal 6-3 and for a second time holding the Redbirds to just six hits"*. Nettie Mae couldn't wait to receive the articles from her son. She would read them to John and then paste them in her scrapbook. One article would tell about Lefty's exceptional controlled pitching, while collecting two more hits than the entire Illinois College team, as he *hurled Illinois Wesleyan to a 10–3 win over the Illinois College Blueboys. The Eureka "lefty" limited Jacksonville to three hits while collecting five on two doubles, two clean singles and an infield hit.* Nettie would also read about Lefty's good friend and teammate Frank Whitman *cracking out a home run in the ninth and later that inning scoring Lefty on a single.*

Not only did Lefty play for Wesleyan but also for one of the local municipal league teams. These games carried great weight in the baseball world during the 1940s. Municipal leagues were a large part of the local entertainment, camaraderie and therapy for returning veterans. Unlike the current subsidized support systems for veterans, the World War II veterans found support wherever they could, and playing ball was one of those supports. With a supervisor or commissioner, the municipal leagues were highly organized at the local and state level. Rules were strictly enforced. Teams recruited and signed local players. The size of the community dictated the league that was authorized to operate: Small towns were considered Class A. Mid-size towns like Bloomington or Peoria were considered Double A, and the larger communities were Triple A. The league sanctioned regional tournaments for league teams according to size. Municipal league teams were funded by community businesses or industries and the teams played for local bragging rights. They often developed a fierce competition and were supported by a large contingent of followers. Families came to cheer on a father, brother, cousin or friend. These leagues were a lifeline for returning veterans as they began to bridge the gap between normal life and the realities of war.

After beginning municipal league play with ISSCS (Illinois Soldiers and Sailors Children's School), Industrial Casualty Insurance recruited Lefty. Lefty notched thirteen wins with the ICI Oilers and clinched the Muny Title during his last season of municipal league play. Wesleyan was well represented within the Muny league with most of the Wesleyan Titans playing for ICI. When the Muny season was complete, three Titans took top honors. It was time to *bring on the 1948 baseball season!* The community read about the Titans' Muny league honors. The *Pantagraph* highlighted that twenty Wesleyan baseball players were waiting for completion of the Bloomington-Normal Municipal League. However, the fellow that really deserved a large part of credit for the team's success was the leagues' *number one moundsman, Dick Van Scyoc.* Van tossed up thirteen wins without a setback. At the close of the season, four jackets were awarded to outstanding performances in league play, with three of those awards going to the Titans. Van received one for his work on the mound.

COACH VAN:

I loved playing baseball and was fortunate that when I entered the service I was afforded the opportunity to play ball. I got opportunities to pitch for base teams. It saved me. I arrived at Illinois Wesleyan University with a stipend of $120 a month and the GI Bill compliments of Uncle Sam. This not only got me admitted to the university, it also paid my way through. I was now a Wesleyan Titan, and to Mr. Young's delight, I became a Sigma Chi. The one unfortunate aspect of entering college as a returning service member in the middle of the school year was the fact that many of us veterans would take team positions from kids who had remained behind during the war or were just entering college. These young players would be sidelined, as returning veterans would take the starting roles with more maturity and a physique that only a war could nurture.

Mr. Young continued to encourage me, and if I needed anything, including a few dollars, he was always willing to help. Every penny Mr. Young loaned me was paid back, including money he had sent me when overseas. It was all written down and given to me when I got my first job. I would do the same with my girls when they got their first jobs. They were given their student loan books, necessary for paying for college, with the understanding that they were capable of paying that loan back. It is empowering for kids to be given responsibilities leading to vital lessons of self-respect and self-determination. This is what Mr. Young and my parents vested in me. This will be something I try to pass on in the years to come.

Fuzz and I married on September 30, 1946. On November 6, 1947, I became a father for the first time. Mr. Young was responsible for naming our first daughter Gwen. Fuzz and I couldn't agree on a name, so when Mr. Young stopped by the hospital, he picked her name from a dozen written on small pieces of paper.

I spent the majority of my time playing ball, working and going to class. With the good ballplayers attending Illinois Wesleyan and with an excellent coach in Jack Horenberger, Wesleyan became known for its excellent baseball program. Often, scouts from the major leagues would be in the stands watching games. A couple of major league teams sent players to Wesleyan for rehabilitation or playing time to keep them sharp while working their way into the line-up. A couple of those players were the White Sox's Cosmidis and Winkles. Winkles kept the team in stitches with his antics. He was from a small town in Arkansas.

We started the season in 1947 by going on a southern trip, playing the likes of Arkansas State, LSU at Baton Rouge, Murray State in Kentucky and then a school in Pensacola, Florida. This was a time that was unprecedented. Boys who thought they were athletes before they left for the war came back stronger and more mature. Soldiers newly released from service and trying to make sense of the last couple of years were returning to schools in record numbers. This meant that current college players were sidelined in deference to newly returning veterans. The Wesleyan Titans were no different, and Mr. Young's write-up about our early southern trip to four different colleges said it all: *"Twenty Players for Southern Trip - Titans Launch New Campaign in Arkansas. With overflowing registrations, many of the boys who have won letters during the war years at Wesleyan are **not** included in the 20 man traveling squad"*.

College ball and municipal league play gave me lots of exposure to major league teams. Fuzz was now expecting our second child. It was approaching the summer of 1949 and I was getting ready to graduate. I had won twelve straight games in the Bloomington Municipal League and doing really well. One of the teams I pitched against was a Saint Louis Cardinal's minor league team, the Decatur Commodores. I was scheduled to pitch the first three innings but ended up pitching the whole game. Every three innings coach kept telling me to keep going. I ended up as the winning pitcher, and from that experience I was invited to pitch batting practice to the Cardinals and work out with them.

When I got to Saint Louis, I saw players like Stan Musial, Joe Garagiola, Enos Slaughter and others in the locker room and around the stadium. Harry Brecheen was the starting pitcher, a left-hander, who was known as "The Cat" owing to his ability to cover bunts. He was among the many stars at the time and was the first left-handed pitcher to win three games in a single world series. As I stepped on the mound in the old Sportsman's Park in Saint Louis, I took a pause. It was a great experience, but I decided to turn down the $275 per month offer to join their minor league team. I would have to claw my way up to the majors. It would have meant a lot of time away from Fuzz and the kids. So I returned to Eureka. I knew playing in the big leagues was no longer my dream. I had a wonderful wife and we were expecting our second child. I settled on coaching and teaching and was excited to begin a new chapter in my life at Hittle High School in Armington, Illinois. I was hired as the new high school basketball coach at a school of sixty students. I would teach physical education, a couple of history classes to seventh and eighth graders and coach basketball.

I would still be able to supervise the junior league baseball program in Bloomington, a program that had grown to over one thousand boys. It was now time to start my career and focus on family.

CHAPTER 5
My Heart, My Friend

From "The Chaos of Stars" by Kiersten White

I didn't fall in love with you,

I walked into love with you,

With my eyes wide open,

Choosing to take every step along the way.

I do believe in fate and destiny,

But I also believe we are only fated to do the things

That we choose anyway.

And I'd choose you; in a hundred lifetimes, in a hundred worlds,

In any version of reality,

I'd find and choose you.

NARRATOR:

I have heard it said that true love might only come once if we are lucky. For Coach Van, he has been fortunate to marry two different women, each of whom celebrated thirty years of marriage with him. In fact, he just celebrated forty years with his second wife, Karen. But we will start with Mary, his high school sweetheart.

It was a remarkable love story of a young high school debutante that stole Van's heart. Her name was Mary Kathryn Frerichs, better known to her friends as Fuzz. They met in a math class, and Van, a year older, offered to help her with her studies. They weathered a long-distance courtship during the war, and then began their married life in 1946 when Van was playing ball for the Illinois Wesleyan Titans while going to school. They had their first child, Gwen, in 1947, but it was their one-bedroom basement apartment that pressed Lefty to think about leaving school. The apartment would flood when it rained, making conditions unbearable. Money was scarce. Lefty told Mr. Young he would have to leave school and get a job to make adequate provision for his young family. Mr. Young took to finding them a decent place to live.

COACH VAN:

Our first apartment in Bloomington was something to behold. It was so bad I knew I had to do something. We were going to move in with Fuzz's father, and I was going to quit school and get a job. I talked to Mr. Young, and he told me to give him a few days. He found us a place in "faculty row". These were apartments rented only to faculty members at the university, but one was vacant. We were approved to move into the apartment, and that was how we came to live in the faculty barracks at Wesleyan. To make ends meet, we rented one of the two bedrooms to a Gene Herman and another student. This brought in an extra $29 per month, and with our rent at $30 per month, we were only out $1.00. Not too bad! Formula, diapers and other baby items added to our expenses. We didn't even have enough money for an ice cream cone; something our renters would eat in front of us every chance they got, or so we thought.

While at Wesleyan, Fuzz worked at State Farm and I attended college. We had an old car that Aunt Althea (Mary's aunt on her mother's side) sold us. We paid a whopping $200 for it; we just never knew when it would run. Fuzz would hustle to the bus stop, a few houses away from our apartment, while I would try to start the car. If it started, she would hurry back and we would drive. If the car didn't start, Fuzz would hold the bus while I ran down the street and hopped on. Those were challenging days. Pat

Van Scyoc, my niece, Frank's daughter, would babysit for us. I was hoping things would improve financially when I graduated.

Right before graduation, I was offered the Bloomington High School assistant coaching job for $2000. I accepted, but it came without living arrangements so I had to find an apartment for us. The $2000 would be tight. So I was going to have to look for additional work to supplement this income. About this same time, Bob Pratt, a father of one of my junior league baseball players, informed me that the little farming community of Armington was looking for a new basketball coach. He thought I would have a great chance at getting the job and wanted me to apply. He set up an interview with the school board, a forty-minute drive from Bloomington-Normal. The clincher was the job came with a rent-free house. I was offered the position and began my first job with a $3800 salary, better than what Bloomington had offered. Bloomington High School let me out of my contract, and Fuzz and I moved to Armington. I was originally going to ask for $3600 but Fuzz told me to ask for $3800, so I did. To my surprise, Mr. Pratt said, "That should be doable!" I said yes and we picked a move-in date. There was only one catch, and Fuzz and I were about to find that out.

When Fuzz and I moved into our new home in Armington, we were surprised that the house didn't have any running water including hot water. The main water came from an indoor pump. In fact, water from the pump was a little unnerving. Every now and then, a black insect would appear out of the pump. Mary refused to use our faucet and would go to the neighbor. The neighbor would come to our house for the same reason, thinking ours was better than hers. The first full summer in Armington we upgraded the plumbing in the house while also putting in a hot water heater.

NARRATOR:

Mary Kathryn, Fuzz, became a big part of Coach Van's coaching life no matter where he was employed. She had attended Knox College for a year and a half in Galesburg until her mother took ill and passed away. Fuzz was quite intelligent and did managerial work while Coach was overseas. When at Armington, she helped with the student council as an advisor. She was at all of the games, often with little Gwen in tow. Nettie had a picture in her scrapbook of little Gwen, hands on hips, smiling at the crowd while doing a cheer with the cheerleaders. Or should we say standing on the court smiling. She was just two years old.

Fuzz was Coach Van's biggest fan at Armington, Washington and for ten years at Manual. At Washington, Coach and Fuzz moved into an apartment above the Romani's. Roy Romani was a teacher and coach at the high school, and would become Coach's best friend. He was leaving the basketball position to move into administration. Coach Van was to replace him as head boys' basketball coach. Roy and his wife, Ada, had three children: Mel, Ron and Diana. Mel and Ron would play basketball for Van. The Van Scyocs moved three additional times while in Washington, the second move to a rental home, and then they purchased their own home, a block from Washington High School at 617 W. Jefferson Street. They eventually sold this home but kept the lot next door and built a new home two years before Coach took the Peoria Manual coaching job.

Coach's home on W. Jefferson Street in Washington was convenient for him and the ballplayers. It was just two short blocks to the high school gym. The players would stop by and pick up the keys to the gym with Coach telling them to lock the door behind them and not let anyone else in. Couldn't do that in today's world, but we're talking small town Washington in the 1950s. Often Coach would be right behind them, give or take ten minutes. Those were good times.

Golden Babcock, Roy Romani, Ray Abernathy, Jack Reeder, Jack Strongberger, Ed Usnik, Bill Bradle and others along with their wives would follow the team, stopping by the Van Scyocs' after home games. It was a time of basketball fellowship with plays examined and future games discussed. Getting together could be to commemorate a win or forget a loss. Fuzz worked to make everyone feel at home. The house was never too clean, nor too messy, but it was always full of activity. Jack Reeder, Van's former player and top assistant, was the one designated by Coach to break up the party and move people out if the hour got too late.

This was a time when holidays were spent in different towns around the state. Different teams would attend different tourneys, and the Van Scyocs were always on the road to Galesburg, Carbondale, and Rockford; just to name a few, and then there was Pontiac. Coach Van had the most history with the Pontiac tourney. To Pontiac's credit, their athletic department made a contribution to Coach Van's endowed scholarship honor at Illinois Wesleyan University in 2007.

During the late 1960s and through the early 70s, the Manual Rams traveled to Carbondale for their Christmas tourney. Coach Van and the family would get up early, open presents on Christmas morning and then hit the road for Carbondale's three-day event. And it never failed that each year snow would make the trip treacherous. Each tourney brought shouting fans, hotel rooms, eating out, shopping between games and lots and lots of basketball. The Van Scyocs were a close-knit crew and all supported Coach. Fuzz never complained. It was a *family affair*. Coach's daughters came to love the game as much as he did. That might be how Coach ended up with two sons-in-law, Bob Bogle and Chuck Westendorf, who; as he often joked, "could do nothing but coach". This he lamented when he needed some help on a project around the house. He would remark, "Neither daughter could marry an electrician or plumber!" He always had fun giving the two a hard time!

Peoria Manual High School was the last move Fuzz made with Coach. They left Washington and their friends of the past fifteen years to start a new chapter in their lives. West Manor Parkway, on the upper West Side of Peoria, became Fuzz's new home, and she settled in to a whole new world. She and Coach lived up the hill from the high school, just a few miles door to door. Peoria was a much larger community than what Fuzz was accustomed. She had to battle a bout of depression while making the transition from small town to big city. But after a while she came to love the people and the city of Peoria as much, if not more than the others. For her, no matter where she was with Coach, it was a place she could call home. Coach was again building a basketball program, this time on the south side of Peoria in a more difficult time. Coach had an interesting perspective on life, people, relationships and communities. He believed that you treat people the way you would like to be treated. He also believed in respect for yourself and others. If something was important to do, then it should be done to the best of your ability. Now he would live his beliefs in a community fraught with differences: racial, economic and cultural. But, if you asked Coach, nothing changed other than location.

Fuzz, as one of the team's most dedicated fans, began supporting the team while developing a relationship with the parents and players. Coach and Fuzz would often stop at Hunt's Drive Inn, a small well-known diner near Bradley Park, after a game just to grab a bite to eat and rehash the action. She got to know assistant coaches. She knew the names of the sportswriters, broadcasters and referees. She spent time with boosters and fans that just wanted to be part of the action. But with all this said, her favorite place to be was on their island in Minnesota, away from the noise and activity that was basketball. And her favorite thing to do was to spend time fishing with Coach when the season ended. In 1976, after a six-month battle with cancer, Fuzz quietly passed away with Coach never leaving her side.

But that wasn't the end of the story, because after a couple of years and some passage of time, Coach was introduced to another woman, bright and full of life. She had two sons that played junior high school ball at Calvin Coolidge. It felt right. He and Karen married in June 1978. She made her home with Coach and her two boys on West Manor Parkway.

Karen learned quickly about Coach's obsession with being on time. Once, she was driving them to Champaign while Coach caught a quick nap. He was to attend the All State Board meeting, to make recommendations on all-state players, before the state tourney began. He woke up in time to see Lake Springfield passing by and realized they had headed south instead of east. He knew they would be late. They pulled over and Coach called Bob Leavitt, a Peoria sportswriter who represented him at the meeting. Karen was officially baptized into Coach's basketball life, and the story has become a favorite to tell. Over the years, Karen weathered the ups and downs of the basketball season. She attended the Illinois Basketball Coaches Hall of Fame Banquets (long banquets) each year in Bloomington, warmed benches of different gyms throughout the state, traveled to summer camps to watch the Rams play summer ball and made sure that Coach always looked his best. She learned how to fish, drive a runabout boat on Lake Vermillion, clean fish and haul water to the cabin in Minnesota on Daisy Island.

Karen lived the struggles of raising two teenage sons while adjusting to married life inside the River City basketball fishbowl! At Manual High School, nothing happened that Coach didn't find out about. One of those times was leaving the boys, Karen's two sons, who were now in high school, home alone for a three-day weekend while he and Karen traveled to California to visit Velma, his niece and one-time backyard baseball buddy. When Karen and Coach returned, everything seemed fine. On the first Monday that Coach was back at school, however, the two boys heard names of their teammates being called to Coach's office one by one. Every time a new name was called, it felt like a noose tightening. Finally, Coach confronted his stepsons. Yes they had had a party at the house and yes it did involve alcohol and yes they did drive the Lincoln all over town and then some. This story of "growing up with Van Scyoc" now brings laughter. Coach will tell you that raising boys is quite a bit different than raising girls. But he loved them no less! Maybe, if they hadn't left the bottles in the trashcan, no one would have been the wiser.

Now, in the dusk of Coach's life, if you stop over at the house on West Manor, Karen will greet you at the front door. She will be impeccably dressed, hair and nails done, jewelry on and a smile on her face. You will see Coach's protector, caregiver, friend, confidant, strength and his happiness all rolled up into one person. She will walk you down the stairs to the TV room. You might catch Coach working out, riding his bike or lifting weights. He might be reading one of his novels or taking a short nap. Whatever the activity, Karen is just a few steps away.

COACH VAN:

God saw fit to bless me with two incredible women in my life. I met my first wife in high school. She caught my attention in geometry. She was having trouble with her assignments, and I offered to help her. Actually, I wanted to get to know this cute little blonde. Her name was Mary Kathryn Frerichs or, as friends and family called her, "Fuzz". She lit up my life. Our relationship grew over time. I finally earned the trust of her parents, Hyung and Verdie Frerichs. Her father was from the old country, an immigrant from Germany. Her mother was a schoolteacher, a well-educated lady. I felt very lucky to be the one Fuzz's mother called when Hyung was stranded in Peoria delivering chickens in an Illinois snowstorm. Hyung owned and ran a chicken farm. Verdie asked me if I could come and keep the furnace going in the chicken barn so the chickens wouldn't die. If they lost the chickens, they would lose their livelihood. I was willing to do anything to increase my stock where Mary Kathryn was concerned, and I felt this would help me in that department.

Fuzz's mom, Verdie, was a praying woman. She attended the Eureka Christian Church, and I know she was praying for me. Fuzz's mom died from cancer at the early age of fifty while I was stationed in Texas. I got a five-day furlough to travel home for the funeral. I caught a ride on a small military plane headed to New York. It was a non-stop flight, but the pilot felt sorry for me and landed in Saint Louis just long enough for me to hop out. I remember the pilot giving me instructions to get out quick, keep my head down and run. The only thing he knew about me was that I was going to a funeral and he went out of his way to help me. I hitchhiked from St. Louis to Eureka. Those things stick with you.

I had great respect for Verdie. She had written me a long letter when I went off to the service. Of all the letters my mom kept, that is the one I wish I had, but it has been lost. Probably because I carried it with me wherever I went while I was overseas. I remember what it said. She told me she would be praying for me and she admonished me to always take care of Mary Kathryn. Unfortunately, history would repeat itself when my beloved Fuzz would succumb to the same disease that took Verdie; cancer, at the same age of fifty. It was only six months from the day that she got ill until the time I lost her. She died October 1; the first day teams were allowed to begin basketball practice in 1976. That was just like my Fuzz. She waited until the first day of the high school basketball season to slip out of this world knowing I would have the players to focus on, a distraction, something I loved to do that would keep me going.

I've learned over time that God doesn't give us more than we can handle, even when it seems like he does. Joy does come in the morning. My morning started when I met Karen Sue Storey Van Waes. She became my second wife, and her sweet, sweet spirit is something I am grateful for every day. Mary Kathryn graced my life in the beginning, helping me during my education and career, while Karen Sue has been by my side during the middle years of that long career and now continues to love me even as dusk approaches. When I met Karen, we talked about having maybe ten or twenty good years together. It is hard to believe we are approaching forty. Karen has been a blessing, never complaining and always putting my needs before her own. Taking care of someone who is ninety-four is not easy, but she does it with tenderness and love.

Karen's two sons are like my own. They played ball for me at Manual. Each one had to walk his own journey living with this no-nonsense, hard-nosed coach. I had to learn to be a father of *high schoolers* again, this time boys. I can only hope they know how important they are to me. I feel fortunate to have known them and to have been able to play a small part in their lives. Danny surprised me at his college graduation by putting "Thanks Coach" on the top of his graduation cap. Everyone in Murray State

University's gymnasium at the commencement was able to see that special note. It meant the world to me and I won't forget it. We still talk about the party the boys had when Karen and I were out of town. The boys tell that story much better than I ever could. And for a while after I retired, the boys would meet me in Duluth, Minnesota, at the start of the summer fishing season, drive us up to Lake Vermilion two hours away and help get the cabin ready for the summer. They took time away from their own families to help me, and it is something that I will always cherish. We had great times telling stories, fishing and lounging around the cabin. To say I have been blessed is an understatement.

CHAPTER 5
HITTLE HIGH

*Choose a job you love and you will never
have to work a day in your life.*
Anonymous

NARRATOR:

Coach had entered the next phase of his life, married, with two little girls under two years of age. He had just been named the new head basketball coach at Armington High School while he continued to manage the Louis E. Davis Junior League baseball program that would swell to one thousand boys from the Bloomington area by the time his tenure ended. Baseball was a big part of Coach's life, and unbeknownst to him at the time, he would spend a lifetime helping shape the character of boys and young men.

One of Coach's former players, David Booth, who works in the front office of the NBA's New Orleans Pelicans, made an interesting observation when discussing his close relationship with the man, "It's like Coach had a ministry or calling that is only understood after the fact and by those of us who put our faith in God". That faith for Coach was unclear in his early development when Nettie would get him ready for Sunday school and send him off by himself on rare Sunday mornings. Nettie had a hard life, and church was intimidating. However, she worked to help her son understand faith, and on occasion she would accompany him. His baptism picture hung on the living room wall.

Fuzz's mom would have a profound effect on the young Van Scyoc, as he saw a woman who was dedicated to her faith and her church. She was a lady of prayer, and Coach observed her battle with cancer, the same struggle his beloved Fuzz would endure. Coach developed a faith that was deep and private. It would be tested when Fuzz died and he would have to slowly learn to trust again. Karen would help him find this resolve and understand that, as he would often say in later years, "God will never give you more than you can handle".

But for now, Coach was at Armington and continued to supervise the Louis E. Davis Post 9 Junior League baseball program in Bloomington during the summer. In fact, the *Bloomington Pantagraph* would run a story on this topic on August 14, 1949, that graced the inside spread of the paper. Coach's picture, towering over a young boy, was on the top right. Under the picture it read: *"Manager Dick Van Scyoc towers over Tommy While of the Benson Ramblers. Tommy was one of the smallest this summer".* The headlines attest to the importance of the program to the community: *"JUNIOR BASEBALL KEEPS BOYS OUT OF MISCHIEF"* The program continues to grow as boys get experience and have fun.

It is a small write-up, framed by twelve multi-sized pictures telling a human-interest story. Pictures are representative of the program and showcase some of the six hundred fifty boys. The boys were aged 9–17 and played their baseball games at Fred Carlton field. Another picture of fifty bicycles parked under a tree in random order is identified with this caption: *"THERE'S A GAME ON – A jam of parked bicycles mark playing days at the Fred Carlton Field. Most boys hooked shoes and glove on handlebars and rode in with one passenger at least".* The article continues: *"Bloomington is experimenting with a cure for boyhood trouble in summer that goes down easier than candy. It's baseball. In a style that probably would have warmed the heart of Charley (Old Hoss) Radbourne, who developed a pitching arm in the barn-lots of Bloomington that carried him into Baseball Hall of Fame at Cooperstown, N.Y."*

So, in the tradition of Charley (Old Hoss) Radbourne, Coach influenced lives and integrated life lessons into athletic completion while entering a different phase in his already accomplished athletic career. The lessons he passed on have built character in young men and women. He became a substitute father to some and a mentor to others. Coach also impacted kids in the classrooms and those who were part of his work-study program. They too learned his life lessons and became better people for having been one of his students. Upon retirement at Manual, Coach became a mentor and friend to young boys in a Pekin junior high school program targeting students with behavioral problems. He worked as a teaching assistant for his daughter Jan. Again, his impact was keenly felt. Mostly, his lessons were learned through basketball, a sport Coach taught at the high school level for forty-five years. It all began in Armington. Here's an article that announced his new position:

"Dick Van Scyoc New Director at Armington

Richard L. Van Scyoc of Eureka, who in the spring signed a contract as assistant coach at Bloomington High School, has been granted a release from his contract at his own request, it was announced Tuesday night by A. Royce Evans, secretary of the board of education. Van Scyoc several weeks ago was tendered the position of athletic director and head coach at Hittle Township High School at Armington and felt it was too attractive an opportunity to pass up and the board did not feel they should stand in the way of his advancement. He will report there at the conclusion of the Southern Illinois university coaching school next Thursday".

Nettie has cut and pasted a couple of short articles in her scrapbook that explain Coach's new coaching duties. The first talks about his first job at Armington. The second gives an account of what his team was doing in preparation for an upcoming game with Morton.

"At Armington we met a new figure in Tazewell county athletics, Dick Van Scyoc, now in his first year of coaching at Hittle Township High School after several successful seasons as a Wesleyan Athlete".

"Dick Van Scyoc and his Armington team scouted the Washington-Morton game Friday. The Mustangs clash with Morton in the opening round of the county tournament Tuesday night, and should they win that one, might face Washington in the semi-finals".

COACH VAN:

Fuzz and I looked forward to the move to Armington. We thought this would be a good place to start the next chapter of our lives and would enjoy making it our home. It was 1949 and money was tight, so I continued to supervise the junior league baseball program in Bloomington. The Armington school board allowed me to take my three summer months' pay in one lump sum for the 1950 school year. This became our down payment on a car I needed to continue my summer employment.

I was fortunate to begin my coaching career at Hittle High school. It was a great place with great people. The school was small, with around sixty students. The only problem with small meant that we didn't have many boys for a varsity basketball team, but the few kids we did have worked hard and were kids of great character. I remember the likes of Charlie Fort, Wendell Nagle, Bob Pratt, Darrell Burt, Wayne Dickerson, Bob Eckhardt, Tom Brandt and Billy Atteberry. I even remember Bill Gaddis, the former Olympia coach. I knew him when he was in diapers and knee pants. My scorekeeper was Bob Israel. We had fourteen wins and twelve losses my first year, 1949–50. Then we went 13–12 in 1950–51. One of our biggest thrills at Hittle High was beating the Morton Potters, a school much larger than Armington. This meant we won the traveling Tomahawk Trophy, a great victory for our little school and a great surprise to Morton. Morton hadn't given us a second thought. But we prepared, went to their home court and came away with a win. Even my youngest daughter Gwen got involved.

70

She was just eighteen months old. But the cheerleaders wanted her to be the mascot, so they put a matching cheer uniform on her. She would keep everyone entertained. It even made the papers: *"BASKET BRAWLS - Little Gwen Van Scyoc, whose daddy coaches Armington's Mustangs, captured the heart of every fan. Dressed like the Armington cheerleaders, Gwen performed like a veteran as assistant to the whooper-uppers".*

That was quite a night and we stopped to celebrate. The kids bought me a well-deserved milkshake, as they put it. I didn't want to admit it, but I couldn't have bought any milkshakes that night, let alone my own. Money in the Van Scyoc household was really tight. But who says you need a lot of money to be happy. These were some of my fondest memories. Knowing that I needed to beef up my knowledge on coaching basketball, I called my good friend Mike Chianakas who was coaching at Dwight, Illinois. He and I sat down to talk x's and o's.

Here's a letter Mike Chinakas (Eureka 1943, Former classmate and teammate) wrote to me on my endowed scholarship honor. *Dear Lefty (Dick)*

I am privileged to be included in this very special honor you are to receive and to be afforded the opportunity to add a remark dating back to our earlier years in Eureka. In fact, I'll no doubt have at least two remarks to burn your ears!

What an inspiration you were to me. As one year older and a class ahead you encouraged me whenever I was substituted for you with "do better than I did". That was, even then as now, a big order to fill – but I tried.

Then the time you accepted your first job at Armington and you called me (a beginner at Dwight High School) to make some time for us to talk about basketball – a subject you later excelled in through your history making 826 wins. And you asked me for advice! How can I forget that a young fellow starting coaching could impart so much wisdom to make you the top man in Illinois High School basketball coaching names! I shall never forget.

If you recall, Frank Whitman and you started baseball in Eureka at the time C.C. Galbreath was our coach. I'm convinced his knowledge of sports was minimal but you took over the "technical" stuff and we played baseball!

What cute little Frerichs girl was in my class and I figured I had an inside track – but no! She ended up dating older men like Dick Van Scyoc. You make a fine couple and deserved one another. Life does take its bounces doesn't it!

I am delighted to drop this letter to Gwen and I thank our Lord every day for the people that have touched my life – especially Dick "Lefty" Van Scyoc. It is so obvious to me that he has been an integral part of yours.

Your "old" friend

George Mike Chianakas

Eureka, Class of '43

(A graduate of Michael's Sweet Shop!)

Next, I made an appointment with one of Illinois' premier coaches, the legendary Duster Thomas of Pinckneyville. I traveled all day to his southern Illinois town to see him and found him on a golf course playing golf. He was eager to help me, a new young coach right out of the gate. We spent a little time talking hoops, but I spent more time listening to him share his basketball philosophy. He talked about the game in general, about kids and how to develop them as a team. He believed in strong discipline and running a tight ship. He was gracious and reinforced my own attitudes and beliefs when it came to the game. I eventually forged my own philosophy over the years, and I would like to think kids are better for having participated in our programs.

In the summer I did what all guys my age were doing: I played baseball for Armington in the Tri-Valley Baseball League. It was a league established in the early months of 1945 by Joe Thierer and others who wanted to provide "community interest in the sport"; similar to the municipal leagues I had played in. I still have the Tri-Valley League rulebook that identifies the board of directors, communities involved, committees, specific rules and teams. The league was very well organized and even instituted contracts that teams and players had to sign. Armington was part of a ten-city league. There were other leagues throughout the state. It was pretty serious stuff. Each town, that had a team, took it seriously and recruited good ballplayers, kids who played college ball and were home for the summer or guys out of college who had played, guys like me. We had a swell time. Fuzz would bring the girls and a blanket and take in the game. The community of Armington was very supportive, and it gave us all a little entertainment during those long hot summers.

I wore a lot of hats my first year at Armington. I was the director of athletics, coached high school baseball and basketball, taught history at the elementary school and even coached seventh and eighth graders. I gave up grade school teaching and coaching my second year. In return, another teacher, Ralph Buck, and I were recruited as co-interim principals at the high school. It so happened that the principal was in a car accident. He ended up in the hospital and mail was piling up. The school board realized bills needed to be paid and mail needed answering, so they tapped the two of us to fill in. We met Bob Pratt, a board member, in the principal's office to learn how to open the safe and pay the bills. It was during this visit we were all mortified to find out the principal was not honoring his commitments. Money was missing. Letters were stored in the safe without being opened. He had not paid any bills. As we dug deeper, we found the principal was fudging on lots of things. Needless to say, when the principal recovered, he did not return to Hittle High, which left Buck and me in charge. Buck and I continued our co-principal duties until the end of the school term. But that wasn't the half of it.

One spring day I was at the baseball field practicing for a game when a student worker came running to get me. She said one of Buck's students had gone berserk and was chasing Buck with a tire iron. I took off running to the high school hoping nothing bad happened. I was horrified to see Buck's car smashed to smithereens. I still hadn't a clue on what was up.

Then out of the corner of my eye, I saw Buck walking up the road. He looked scared to death and kept looking over his shoulder. He told me that one of his students started an argument. He couldn't even remember what it was about. The argument escalated, but then the student just left. Buck saw him go to his car, so he thought the student was going home. But instead he returned with a tire iron and threatened Buck. Buck ran at that point. He was just coming back when I saw him. We concluded the student must have taken his anger out on Buck's car. He sure did a good job. Buck and I called the police. When they got to school, they took all of Buck's information and then told us to be careful until they got hold of this kid. They would let us know what happened. Buck was still on edge when I left for the day.

When I got to school the next morning, Buck met me at the door and said he wanted to show me something. He took me into the principal's office we shared. He proceeded to the desk and opened the top left drawer. He then pulled out a small 38-caliber handgun. I hadn't seen a gun since the service. "Wow! Put that away" was all I could say. He put it back in the drawer and told me if I needed it I would know where to find it. I was just hoping this student wouldn't return. If he had, I think Buck would have shot him. We were lucky. He never returned to school. This is what you call learning on the job.

I had great kids at Armington. The community supported Fuzz and me and made us feel welcome. I was not the only coach to begin his career at Hittle Township High School. Coach Joe Stowell, Bradley University's men's head basketball coach for thirteen seasons, followed me to the halls of Hittle High when I left to take the Washington job!

NARRATOR:

Coach continues to have fond memories of Armington. It was hard for Fuzz to leave the friends she had made when they entertained the idea of moving to Washington. The Washington School Board made the young coach an offer; and even though it meant a $2000 pay cut, he felt the opportunity was one he couldn't pass up. Coach came highly recommended even with an average winning percentage of just over 500, for his two years at Hittle High. But Armington had beaten Morton on Morton's home court and this was something that made other schools in the area take notice. Coach would frame his move this way: "The difference between Washington and Armington, was the running water". Coach turned in his keys and walked out of Hittle Township High School in the summer of 1951 for the last time. He and Fuzz had no idea what awaited them.

Coach wouldn't leave Hittle High with a bare cupboard. He left Armington in good hands. They hired a new, young Bradley University graduate, Joe Stowell, to take over. Coach and Stowell's paths would cross often, and they would form a close friendship. Stowell would recruit many of Coach's players to come to Bradley.

A letter, written to Coach on his endowed scholarship honor, follows:

JOE STOWELL: (Former Bradley University Men's Basketball Coach)

Dear Coach Van:

It was to be my first interview for a teaching job and I didn't have a clue as to what to expect when I drove into Armington with my fiancé (Marilyn) in the Spring of 1951. I thought that probably the best thing I could do was to ask some questions of the previous coach, Dick Van Scyoc, who was moving on to a bigger job at Washington.

He gave me several good ideas and during the course of our conversation I asked Dick what he thought I should ask for a salary. I believe he said he was making $3,000 or $3,200. I took it from there.

Dick lived a block from the high school and when I arrived I found they were going to interview six people that night and we all sat in a school desk in the study hall. I was 5th to be interviewed by the school board, which took place in the principal's office. I was asked a number of questions as to why I wanted the job, my religion, how I would handle certain possible discipline problems, etc.

Finally, after about 20 minutes I was asked what I expected for a salary. Remembering what Coach Van had said, I said I thought perhaps $2800 would be fair. One of the board members who appeared to be the most out-spoken then said that so and so said he would take it for $2600. I probably replied too fast, as I said, "Well, I guess he should know what he is worth". Upon returning to my car, Marilyn said, "How did it go", and I said, "It probably went". About a half hour after I got home they offered me the job.

Jim and Jon played for Coach Van and Jerry Coached with him, and all are better people for it. I felt very fortunate to have a large number of his players play for me at Bradley. Congratulations on many jobs well done Coach Van. I feel very fortunate to be numbered among your many friends.

Joe Stowell

Men's Basketball Coach

Bradley Braves (Retired)

CHAPTER 6
WACOHI

*Perfection is not attainable, but if we chase perfection
we can catch excellence.* (Vince Lombardi)

NARRATOR:

The pages of Nettie's old scrapbook are brittle and worn with age. Nettie's devotion to her son can be seen in how faithfully she attended to these books. She and John were living in California and had only the local Illinois newspapers to keep them close to their son. Coach Van sent the papers weekly; but due to Nettie's advancing age, the years and seasons began to merge together. Articles are pasted in random order with different years and different seasons appearing together. It was as though Nettie was having trouble making sense of the timeline by which to place and paste the articles. Seasons were quickly slipping by.

She and John enjoyed reading about Van's basketball exploits; their youngest son, her only child to graduate from college, the one who Nettie readied for Sunday school and for whom she so lovingly baked angel food cakes. Nettie Mae fondly remembered the time that she and John packed their old Ford Model T (Hoopie) for the trip to Illinois. In fact, they would make two trips to Illinois. First to Coach's wedding and then three years later they would attend his graduation. Each time, they were beaming from ear to ear. They found it amusing that their son didn't think the old car would make it. Or maybe he thought they couldn't navigate the trip.

Nettie now had additional articles to be cut and pasted in her old scrapbooks, like the memories she had tucked away in her mind. It would be the final season of her life. The scrapbook clippings are arranged with no cohesiveness or ebb and flow. Toward the back of the big black book, on the left side, is a newspaper headline that highlights one of Coach's pitching exploits from an earlier time: It reads, *"WESLEYAN TAKES THRILLER FROM STATE NORMAL, 3-2; VAN SCYOC SHADES PAULSON IN GREAT PITCHING DUEL".* On the following page, an article is pasted with a picture of a pretty girl and underneath the caption reads, *"Miss Frerichs: Eureka Girl to Marry Mr. Van Scyoc. The Wedding will be Sunday, September 1, 1946".* Moving to the right is another article announcing Coach's decision to take the men's head coaching job at Washington Community High School. The year written on the article is 1951:

"Richard L. Van Scyoc, coach and physical education teacher of Hittle township high school, Armington, has accepted a contract from the Washington community high school board of education, District 308, for a similar position here this coming school year.

Coach van Scyoc, who received his bachelor of philosophy degree from Illinois Wesleyan University, Bloomington, in 1949 . . . a native of Eureka, he attended high school there, earning four letters in football and baseball and three in basketball. He was active in baseball at Illinois Wesleyan. He will serve as basketball and baseball coach at the local school, assist in football and teach physical education".

Nettie continued to faithfully catalogue articles, even while her son moved on to a new phases in his career. He took the reins at Washington High School and now had the ability to compete with the big boys, schools like Peoria Central, Pekin and Galesburg. This didn't happen right away; but Coach set his sights on building a premier program, and this included playing these top-notch teams. The year was 1951. Washington was just forty miles north of Armington and a stone's throw east of Eureka, Coach's hometown. The first test for Van, as the Panther's head coach, was against his old hardwood crew at Armington. Joe Stowell would turn in an impressive first year record of seventeen wins as Van's replacement. But one win he couldn't get was against Van and the Washington Panthers. He just could not out hustle the twenty-eight-year old Coach and his new Washington club. Washington beat Armington in the county tourney match-up, 35–24. The newspaper covered the game:

"Dick Van Scyoc packed too many guns for his former pupils as eight of 10 men he employed scored in the slow-moving contest . . . After Jack Reeder's free throw broke a 10 all tie with two minutes remaining the panthers were never headed. Reeder, Don Blair, Katy Heavrin, and Dale Sommers all connected to spark the Panther surge".

It was a bittersweet win for Coach as he had forged great friendships with his kids and the people of Armington. This would remain true over the years. Coach Stowell, who was now the head coach at Hittle High, would eventually end up at Bradley University as the head boys' basketball coach.

Coach's first season at Washington ended with thirteen wins and twelve losses. It quickly improved during the 1951–52 season, and by the time the year 1953 rolled in, the team was at the beginning of what would be a record-setting 101 wins to just 12 losses over a three-year period. This three-year record still stands. Players established themselves and their names became ingrained in Washington basketball history: names like, Joe Broz, Kayton Heavrin, Tom Adams, Jerry Graff, Jack Reeder, Jim Funk, Ralph Cherrie, Ed Tully, Dale Summers, Mel and Ron Romani, Clark Pool, Virg McElfresh, Steve Gresham and Dave Dearth, just to name a few.

In 1963, Coach Van received a letter from one of his former players, Ed Tully (Class of '53). It had been more than ten years since Tully had played for Coach Van; and it was letters like this one, that made it through his tough exterior, and grabbed at his heart:

10-19-63

From Ed Tully (Class of 53)

Danville, VA

Dear Dick:

I just happened to be thinking today that it has been ten years since I was senior at Washington High School. If anyone had told me then what I am doing today, I wouldn't have believed them, nor would anyone else. As a matter of fact, you could have gotten odds that I would be in prison today instead of putting people there. As best I can recall, ten years ago today, I probably was running cross-country out to a farm past the Central School. I would imagine that it is safe to relate to you now that I used to run half way, stop, and wait for the others to go on and return, then rejoin them for the jaunt back to school. I never was much for physical fitness, then or now.

I am presently in Danville, VA. Having been sent down here in June for the racial situation. I will be here for another six months or so then I will be transferred to another Division. I hope that it is a little closer to home. However, I am expecting to be sent to Birmingham Alabama. Even so I am planning to take my vacation up at the lake next summer, if it is possible. I would imagine that you have started basketball practice by this time, if you wish to tell them something that is positively true, tell them what you told me ten years ago, that is, "You never remember the games that you win, only those that you lose", and "always give your best efforts and you'll never regret having lost". Ten years after having won fifty and lost five, the only ones I can remember are those games in which I didn't do well as I should have and the five that we lost. I hope that you have a good year.

Write if you get a chance.

Sincerely, Ed Tully.

COACH VAN:

Ed Tully was one of my Washington players. He was a great guy, and we stayed in touch. He just recently passed away. He wrote the above letter to me when he was on the job, ten years after graduating from Washington High School. I got a letter in 2006 from Ed congratulating me for having a scholarship endowed at Wesleyan in my name. It was quite an honor. I received quite a few letters from former players including Dave Dearth, Clark Pool, Mel Romani, Gene Thrailkill, Fred Hensey, Don Kelly, Roger Wind (team manager), Ken Wenzel, Ken Meischner, Steve Gresham, Marty Martin (a cheerleader) and many others who contributed to and/or came to the celebration. The phone calls, letters and visits warmed my heart. I stay in touch with lots of my players, and they never cease to amaze me.

I had one player at Washington, Joe Broz, who was probably one of the hardest working players I have ever coached. Joe was a young, gangly freshman in 1953. He tried out for the freshman team, but got cut. Because he was such a hard worker, I asked him to stay around as my manager. He accepted but wanted to know if he could still work out with the team, lift weights, and participate in shooting drills. I said sure as long as he got his job done. Joe had a great work ethic. He actually pushed the other players to step up their game. As he worked out with the team, his skills began to improve. He hoped to make the team his sophomore year.

As team manager, Joe had to be at practice early. He had to sweep the floor, get the basketballs out and check them for air. He was responsible for the gear and other odd jobs. One of his jobs was moving large packages and equipment off the gym floor. We had only one gym at Washington in the early 60s. It was located near a small parking lot on Jefferson Street where school deliveries were made. These deliveries included large boxes of books and other items along with miscellaneous equipment; all were deposited on the gym floor. Often when we arrived for practice, we would find one or more of these types of deliveries waiting for us. We had to move everything to the hall before we could practice. I told Joe to wait for the other guys to arrive before moving the large boxes or furniture, but Joe was resourceful and independent. He wanted to get the job done so he could practice shooting before the other players arrived.

When there was a school play, band concert or some other kind of production on the stage (also located in the gym), Joe would have to pick up rows and rows of chairs that were set up for the event. The gym doubled as our auditorium. The janitors didn't always get the hundred or more chairs picked up before we needed to practice, so Joe did it without complaining. He would pick up trash or anything else that came up. Then he would begin his regime of footwork, layups and shooting.

Joe definitely made an impact on his teammates and me. His dedication and hard work were infectious. He worked hard on his skills his freshman year and then tried out as a sophomore. Again, he failed to make the team, but he didn't quit. He started his routine again. When his junior year rolled around, he had grown, gotten stronger and improved his skill. He made the team but broke his ankle right out of the gate. He sat out most of the season, and it wasn't a productive year for him. Then as a senior, Joe became one of our greatest assets. I knew he would make some university program a great player.

Without any interest from colleges or universities, Joe walked on at Purdue University. Purdue kept him on the roster but with no scholarship. While at Purdue, the Naval Academy, who was there for a game, observed Joe warming up and knew about his story and his situation; that he wasn't a scholarship player. They inquired about him knowing he was a walk-on. Coaches from the Naval Academy pursued Joe and offered him a full ride to play basketball. Joe transferred to the Academy and played four years. His team made it to the first round of the NIT (National Invitational Tournament). It was televised and we got to see Joe play and contribute, even though the picture was black and white and snowy. Joe had great experiences and opportunities because of his hard work and dedication. I wasn't surprised to see him become an officer in the United States Navy. He was deployed on a destroyer. He was a fine young man who wasn't afraid to work hard and follow his dream. I still have the letter I wrote for Joe trying to get him a college scholarship. Interestingly, the letter was addressed to Stan Albeck.

Dear Stan:

Sorry I have put off answering your letter, but you know how things are during basketball season. Joe Broz is a senior and really is 6'6". Joe is only 17 and should grow another inch or two. As far as basketball ability is concerned he is just beginning to look like the player I hoped he would be. He broke a bone in his foot in November and missed a good month. This caused him a slow start. He has been averaging twenty points a game for the past five or six games. Joe has a variety of shots as he can drive and also shoots very well with a jump shot from 15 to 20 feet out. Right now his biggest weakness is defense. This boy is a very willing worker and worked two and three hours a day this past summer on his own so he could play this year. At the present time, he is interested in Purdue, but if he could get a good scholarship I know he would be interested in talking with you. Joe is a good student and wouldn't have any trouble with regards to grades. If I can be of any other help to you, don't hesitate to write to me.

Sincerely,

Coach Van Scyoc

March 9, 1957, the *Chicago Daily News* sports section included a small piece on Joe Broz under "The State Roundup" section:

"*Joe Broz, 6 foot, 6 inch Washington High School Center, played his first full year of basketball this winter despite the fact he is a senior. Broz was Coach Dick Van Scyoc's manager as a freshman, couldn't make the team as a sophomore and was sidelined with a broken foot his junior year*".

Lloyd Armstrong (Sportswriter for the *Pekin Times*) also wrote about Broz (1961): "*Washington: Basketball fans, still rejoicing over their state-bound*

Panthers Saturday, had another reason to be happy. Ex-Washington star Joe Broz started for Navy in the NIT televised game Saturday afternoon. We were watching that with Dick Van Scyoc and you didn't have to watch too closely to tell that Dick was mighty proud. As we remember hearing it. Broz was the only Navy player whose hometown was given in the pre-game introduction"

When we moved to Washington, we rented an apartment above Roy Romani and his wife Ada. Roy had three kids: Mel, Ron and Diana. Ron was the same age as our oldest daughter Gwen. Mel and Ron played for me. Mel was the first all-American in both basketball and football from Washington High School. He played two sports at the University of Illinois his freshman year, and then made the decision to concentrate on football the following three seasons. Ron, Mel's younger brother, played at Murray State University in Kentucky, the same school my two daughters attended. When the kids were young, Roy and I would drive them to the Eureka golf course for some good old-fashioned sledding during those snowy Illinois winters. He was always ready to have a good time. Roy was diagnosed with cancer in 1965 and passed away shortly thereafter. It was a time of great sadness for me, as Roy had become one of my best friends.

We purchased our first home on Jefferson Street, a couple of blocks from the high school, a year or so after moving to Washington. This was a major decision, and I had to take my twelve-month salary over nine months to pay our bills. I got a summer job to cover summer expenses. It was while living on Jefferson Street that the basketball program began to really take hold. We would begin a winning tradition that would take us to the Elite Eight in 1962. My early teams were filled with great kids who worked hard and laid the foundation for the youngsters coming up. One of those players was Tom Adams who was the first player from Washington, Illinois, to become an all-American and have his number retired. The quote by his yearbook picture said it all: "He was capable of imagining all, of arranging all, and of doing everything". He played for the University of Illinois and graduated in 1960. He was named to the 1955–56 All State team and played on the north all-American basketball squad of 1956. Tom served in the navy for two years with the rank of Lieutenant. He died an untimely death at the age of twenty-nine from Hodgkin's disease, leaving a wife and daughter. He was a great man.

Another name that comes to mind is Ralph Cherrie. My memory of Ralph has to do with a young gangly student in my physical education class who became a great ballplayer. A unique situation arose in my PE class. I had to step out of class for a few minutes so I put Ralph in charge, someone I was sure I could trust to keep order. When I came back into the gym, he told me that one of the kids got out of line so he had to smack him! I was caught off guard, never thinking that Ralph would actually smack another student. He took his job seriously. Getting fired quickly crossed my mind. A lesson learned.

The *Journal Star* ran a story about our first Pontiac tournament and focused on two players: Jerry Graff and Tom Adams. The article wasn't about our on-floor play; but rather, highlighted that the reason we didn't stay in a motel in Pontiac was because of the height of these two players. According to this article, the Pontiac motels didn't have beds long enough to accommodate the two players. Although that was not the reason we chose to drive an hour and thirty minutes one way to the three-day affair, we didn't correct the story. On game day, a teams start time depended on whether they advanced to the winners' or losers' bracket. We chose to drive so our players could sleep in their own beds. If we played an extremely early game, we might get hotel rooms for our kids, otherwise we drove.

One change I made early, while at Washington, was conference play. I move the Washington Panthers from the Illini Conference to the larger Cornbelt Conference. The Cornbelt conference was comprised of Normal Community High School, University High School, Bloomington Trinity Catholic High School and Clinton High School. Then I scheduled a tough non-conference schedule picking up Pekin, Galesburg, Peoria Central and Pontiac, along with any others I could coax into our schedule. It changed a bit from year to year, and it paid off. We began to hold our own against powerhouse teams and we began to improve. This didn't mean the community was in favor of the move. They liked winning and winning by big margins; however, I wanted to see what we could do when we played against stiffer competition. I felt it would make our players better.

NARRATOR:

The first year at Washington tested Coach's patience with a record of 13–12 and much inconsistency. This, however, was similar to his start in Armington. The headlines tell the story: *"Panthers Open Net Card With 43-39 Win Tuesday"*, *"Panthers Lose Close One, 52-50, to Gridley Tuesday"*, *"Panthers Last Rally Takes Dunlap, 41-35"*, *"Washington Nips Tremont, 43-39"*, *"Panthers take Third in County Tourney- Down Morton 50-48 in Overtime"*, *"Washington Dumps Washburn- Funk, Summer Count 22"*.

The sportswriters dissected the game writing about players like Okie Baxter, Jack Reeder, Kayton Heavrin, Don and Dave Blair, Ralph Cherrie, Paul Sizemore, Ed Tully, Dale Summers, Jimmy Funk and Fred Weeks. It was a senior ballplayer, Jack Reeder, who had a dramatic impact on Coach Van. Reeder returned to Washington after graduating from Eureka College as Coach's top assistant. These two forged a unique relationship and strong bond. Jack Reeder would be hired to replace Coach Van in 1966.

The 1952–53 campaign ushered in dramatic improvements as players changed. It was now Adams, Graff, Thrailkill, Faubel, Messmer and Dixon heading the campaigns and filling the sports pages. These players wrote a new history for the Panther basketball program, one that won't be matched. From 1952–56 these players began a run of 101 wins to just 12 losses. Toward the end of the 1955 run, a game between the Panthers and Peoria Central's Lions played at Trewyn Gymnasium on Peoria's south side was highlighted in the *Mirror, Washington High School's yearbook.*

"It's a Season to Remember

The team loses to Peoria Central 52-54 yet it could not overshadow such thrilling moments as the victory over Jacksonville, Gerry Graff's scoring record of 102 points at the Pontiac Tourney and his single game record of 42 points against Robinson, our crushing victory over Metamora 112-30 and our Tazewell Tourney Championship. We had a crushing defeat of undefeated Ronoake in the first game of the Regional at Bradley Fieldhouse. At this time, Coach Van Scyoc has only 7 defeats since his first year at Washington until now, an excellent job".

The success the Panthers generated cultivated new talent. It was a personal loss for Coach Van that tempered his enthusiasm.

COACH VAN:

Mom and Dad always looked forward to receiving the local newspapers, and I knew Mom read every word. She had been clipping articles since I was in grade school. She had quite a collection of scrapbooks, and she wasn't stopping. During the summer months, Fuzz and I would take off for California as soon as school let out. One trip, I stopped in Tulsa, Oklahoma, and made a call to Manual High School to decline a job offer. That was in 1956. It took me until Tulsa to decide if I should move to Peoria or stay in Washington. The timing wasn't right to move. The drive usually took four or five days, but we made it in three because I drove day and night. Fuzz would spell me for a while, or we would stop at a roadside diner and I would sleep while the kids and Fuzz got something to eat and killed some time. Mom and Dad loved seeing the kids. Mom always had strawberry shortcake for the girls the minute we arrived. It became something of a tradition.

Now I was driving to California with Harold and Frank during the school year. Mom had been diagnosed with cancer and she was not doing well. We got to spend some time with her, just the three of us boys. It would be the following summer she would pass away. We were all with her. Dad would stay in Washington for a time, but he wanted to return to his home in California. Velma lived close and would look in on him.

NARRATOR:

Fuzz would inherit the scrapbooks. Nettie wanted her to have them, and as Fuzz looked through each book, she could see the articles about Eureka high school, Legion ball, and the war. Nettie had additional books for Wesleyan, Armington and Washington. It was amazing to see the hard work Nettie undertook to keep this written record. Now it was Fuzz's turn. The last article that Nettie Mae pasted in her scrapbook read: *"Washington, Illinois basketball under the direction of a new head Coach named Dick Van Scyoc"*.

Fuzz began gathering newspaper articles about the 1961 team, a team that would win Washington's first regional since 1911. The 1962 team was also special and made the Elite Eight with a 25–3 record. They were one of eight teams to vie for the state title that year. Names like Tom and Dave Kelly, Virg McElfresh, Clark Pool, Carl Meurn and others caught the attention of sportswriters.

"WASHINGTON MAKES 'SWEET 16': TREMONT THEN PEKIN TOUGHEST OPPONENTS SO FAR-VAN SCYOC". Under this headline is a 4 × 5 picture that graces the upper right corner of a happy Mary Kathryn kissing Coach Van smack on the lips. The caption reads: *"Coach's Reward: Only one of the 5,500 fans in Bradley's Robertson Fieldhouse Friday night who could've been anyway near as happy about Sweet 16 berth as Washington Coach Dick Van Scyoc, was his wife Mary and she showed her appreciation as she greeted Dick on the Fieldhouse playing floor in full view of the other 5,499"*. Another writer penned this: *"PANTHERS' 1ST State Trip Since '11 Easiest Yet"*. The *Champaign News Gazette* wrote: *"Washington Wins, Qualifies for 'Sweet Sixteen'; Panthers, Pontiac vie Here Tuesday; I'm Tremendously Proud Lauds Panthers' Van Scyoc; Looking for a Long Shot? Washington Has Outside Chance"*. *Pekin Times* focused on

"Big Civic Sendoff in Washington; Panthers Play Quincy at 9:30, Panthers Vowed after Losing to Mason city in Sweet 16 (by Lloyd Armstrong); *Fans Jam Washington Square for Noisy 'Elite 8' Sendoff".* The final article reads

"Washingtonians turned out by the 100's early Thursday evening to send their beloved Panthers on their way to Champaign. The fire truck led the way from the west, once around a square bulging with cheering fans and on out to the east along U.S. 24 as far as Eureka . . ."

Stretch Miller, a Peoria broadcaster, was the Master of Ceremonies as the team returned home. Washington's Mayor Guedet honored Coach Van and the team, presenting them with the key to the city. Over two thousand people gathered at the town square to take in the festivities.

While Coach was at the helm of the Panthers; and excitement continued to build, so too did pressures and time commitments. Fuzz's dedication to the team remained, but she began to take a break from attending each game. The pressure had taken its toll. During the 1962 season, Fuzz opted to stay home for more challenging opponents. Coach understood and he called her as soon as the game ended. The *Pekin Times* caught a glimpse of their relationship, as the sportswriter penned the following after Washington's super sectional win: *"Washington Coach Dick Van Scyoc interrupted his appraisal of his team's comeback to ask someone to 'to call my wife.' Dick explained: 'She can't take these games, but I told her I'd call right after it was over.'"* Coach, in the same article, heaped praise on his Elite Eight Panthers who had just upset the No. 1 rated Limestone Rockets. *"'I knew you could do it,' he shouted trying to be heard in the bedlam. 'I think toughening up our schedule is responsible for the way we played against East Peoria and Limestone. I have been criticized for such a tough schedule, but it's paid off, finally.'"*

The *Champaign News Gazette* sports reporters reiterated Coach's method for improving his team's chances to make it to state by *"beefing up competition"* and talked about their underdog status telling the Washington faithful *"Take Washington if you are looking for a long shot at the Illinois*

Prep Basketball scramble at Champaign this weekend. The Panther's aren't too big and they're not too fast but their record is 25-2 and that's not bad . . . Coach Dick Van Scyoc pointed for this crack at the tournament five years ago and maybe his timetable might pay off. Van Scyoc pulled his team out of the Illio Conference for just this sort of thing. There was some criticism at the time because the townspeople liked their team's winning ways in the conference of small schools".

According to sportswriter Lloyd Armstrong, *"Jim Gresham, Virg McElfresh, Tom Kelly, Dave Dearth, and junior, Clark Pool made a vow that they would return and win the Sweet Sixteen. The five made this a pledge after their 1961 loss to Mason City in the super sectional".*

Fuzz continued to chronicle the team's success and tell the story of the 1964, '65 and '66 teams. News articles were filled with the exploits of players like Reeves, Pierantoni, Hathcock, Meischner and Alexander. It was during this time period that a young Bob Knight, assistant for West Point, visited and spent the night at the Van Scyocs, invited by Coach Van. He never missed an opportunity to talk basketball. Knight was in town to watch a young Ron Hathcock play ball, but Hathcock could not make the cut owing to a heart murmur that was revealed during his physical. But Coach's offer of a bed and home cooked meal for the night appealed to Knight.

It would also be a time in which Coach had his first controversy with moving a young sophomore player to a starting role. Ken Meischner, a sophomore, was tapped for a starting guard position because of his talent and skill. Seasoned players and parents found this hard to take. It meant an upperclassman was sidelined. For whatever reason, Meischner received death threats and they appeared credible. Notes were left on his car in the high school parking lot. Coach talked to Ken's parents and even suggested that Ken not play in the upcoming game against the East Peoria Red Raiders in light of specific threats. The game was held at East Peoria and Kenny was adamant that he would play. He was a tough young man. Police were in attendance, and it was a tense time. Coach and Ken's parents were uneasy and jumped at every buzzer or loud sound. There were more police on duty than was normal. Only a close-knit group of people knew what was going on. Luckily, nothing happened during the game. Over time the threats ceased. Ken went on to have a very successful career at Washington, and then was recruited and played at Bradley University. Ken ended up on Coach Van's coaching staff at Manual. Ken wrote Coach a very personal letter when he was honored with an endowed scholarship at Wesleyan. The letter is included below. They have stayed in close contact over the years.

KEN MEISCHNER: (Class of 1966)

Dear Coach Van,

I wanted to share a special moment that had a profound effect on me. You may not remember this but it was when I was a freshman. Remember a 5'6", scrawny 120 lbs. WaCoHi student with hopes of playing for Coach Van Scyoc. Jerry Essington was the freshman coach. On Saturday morning we were to tryout; in fact it was the lasts cuts for the freshman team. Now, you have to remember-I came from John Hensey School in Sunnyland where your wife worked. When I was an eighth grader, I use to ask her every day during basketball season how the panthers were doing. She kept me informed. I looked forward to the day I could play at Washington High School. We didn't have a lot of money, especially for extra things, but my mom and dad sacrificed to get me a brand new pair of shoes to tryout for the team. That particular Saturday, as I got ready for tryouts, my shoes were gone. One of the other players stole them. I later found out it was actually one of my for-mer teammates from Sunnyland. Anyway, if you remember the old gym at Washington, I was down stairs in the hallway near that dungy room that had the toilet in it. I was explaining to coach Essington that I would not be able to try out. I can still hear your voice – "Miesh". "Miesh". It was real quiet when I heard that voice. Upon my surprise, as I moved toward the voice, you were sitting on the toilet. You simply said, "What size do you wear?" I told you I wear and 8 ½. You proceeded to take off your shoes and said, "Here, wear these". I don't know if you also remember that I told this story when I was asked to introduce you a few years ago at Phi Delta Kappa. Here you were the Head Coach and Athletic Director of Washington Community High school, taking time to help a small kid from Sunnyland. Coach, I will never forget you and I will always carry this fond memory with me. Have a great day and know how much you have meant to so many.

Ken Meischner (class of 66)

COACH VAN:

During our 1961 and 1962 tournament runs, Fuzz and I would end up having coffee in our kitchen with two sports radio personalities, Lee Ranson and Ron Thorn. They were announcers on radio station WPEO 1020 and would show up in a red station wagon decked out with the station call letters and the words "BIG RED". As we hit a winning streak, it seemed they camped out on our front lawn and would do a live interview in our kitchen every Friday.

The players had their own way to add a little levity to the season. They began to play music in the gym dressing room, and we took that music with us to Huff gym and the state tournament. It made Lloyd Armstrong's write-up. He chronicled how Belleville played Civil War marching songs in the locker room before their game with Centralia, during their super-sectional. Then he pointed out how the Washington Panthers had a five-year ritual of playing music in the locker room before their games. This particular year, our kids listened to Little Richard and Chuck Berry's "Twist" and the "U.S. Bonds". Jack Reeder along with the kids told me it helped them relax, and I bought it hook, line and sinker.

Jack was my right-hand man and I couldn't have gotten along without him. We had some great times together, and he was so willing to do anything to help the team.

Because Jack scouted for us, he missed all of our tournament games until we got to Champaign. He was a team player and was willing to do what was needed for our success.

I was surprised and pleased that our community passed a bond referendum for a new gym after the 1962 season. I had been at Washington for fifteen happy years, and I wasn't looking to go anywhere. My youngest daughter was a junior in high school and was elected president of the student council her senior year. Fuzz was a substitute teacher at Beverly Manor, and our older daughter was a freshman at Murray State University. We spent our summers in Minnesota except for the week that we attended the Indiana-Kentucky all-star game. Rules prohibited coaches from having gyms open in the summer. It was the spring of 1966 when the phone rang. I answered it and spoke to Mr. Ed (Hamm) Weldin, the principal at Peoria Manual High School. He was looking for a new basketball coach and was hoping I would come speak with him about the position. I did.

NARRATOR:

Fuzz added another article to her scrapbook. It is about the last athletic banquet Coach attended at Washington. The headline read, "*Teamwork Crucial in Life, WaCoHi Athletes Are Told*". Coach Van can be seen standing with Dike Eddleman, one of the greatest athletes the state of Illinois has ever produced. Young players who have won awards are showcased. The Bob Neuman Plaque for Sportsmanship was awarded to Larry Brown. The Newman Plaque is in memory of a young Bob Neuman, Coach Van's former teammate who played with the Eureka 9 Junior League in 1941. The award is given in his honor after his untimely death from drowning. For Coach Van, it is a special award given in honor of his friend.

This awards banquet was at the end of the 1965 campaign, the twentieth annual Washington High School Athletic Banquet hosted and the last one Coach Van would attend as the head coach of the Panthers. Dike Eddleman, the invited speaker for the event, highlighted teamwork and the life lessons athletics teaches. He spoke about the importance of sports and how athletics can inform a player's life, as it requires those players to make critical decisions in a split second. Athletic competition requires young athletes to trust their teammates. Playing forges strong character that is grounded in hard work, determination and commitment to something bigger than oneself. Eddleman went on to say that participating in athletic competition can make you a better person. He ended with a quote from Arthur A. Trout, his old coach and mentor from Centralia High School: "What I gave, I have. What I didn't give, I've lost forever". Eddleman, much like Coach Van, saw success in helping others achieve their potential. Coach presented basketball and baseball awards to his players. He knew he would no longer be working with these athletes, kids he had come to know and care about. He told the crowd that he regretted having to leave Washington, but he emphasized the many happy and productive years he had with the Washington Panthers and the high school. Fuzz didn't attend the banquet. She was happy for Coach but a little sad at having to say good-bye to so many friends. It was hard. Was this choice a good choice? They were about to find out.

CHAPTER 7
SUNSET

Sometimes you will never know the true value
of a moment until it becomes a memory.

NARRATOR:

Summer was always the best of days, especially at Sunset Island in Minnesota. There were no gyms to go to, no practice and no games. Rather, Coach got to enjoy the lake: change the water in the minnow bucket, gas up the outboard motor for the runabout and make sure the fishing boat was ready to go. It was a simple time. There was no electricity, no television and very little radio, depending on if the kids could actually pick up a station. It was a time to do family things even if the family wasn't always on board. As the girls got older, they weren't as anxious to leave their friends and spend three months on an island located seven miles from a mainland and civilization. Coach liked it that way, as he didn't have to worry about his girls and their social lives, at least not during the summer.

These were days filled with fishing, swimming, water skiing, sitting by a night time fire and just whittling away time. The evenings might include popcorn the old-fashioned way, popped in a skillet with grease and popcorn, hoping it didn't burn. Nothing was wasted on Sunset, because a grocery run meant a twenty-minute boat ride before the forty-five-minute car ride to the nearest grocery store. The one thing the Van Scyocs could count on, as a family, was lots of laughter and a close family bond that was unbreakable.

COACH VAN:

I bought an Island on a lake that has 313 miles of shoreline and is 35 miles in length. Currently, I have a bird's eye view from my cabin's deck, of what's happening in the bay that makes up my front yard. The public marina that sits on the opposite side of that bay is continually busy with fishermen launching their boats, while entering and leaving this pristine piece of paradise. The water is clear, the air fresh and we get a soft breeze right off the lake. I love to fish, and when I was younger, I did a lot of it. Not so much anymore. The loons seem to talk to me in their unique bird lingo every morning. I can catch a view of deer, maybe a porcupine and some-times a bear in the woods right near the cabin. We've been known to be foster parents to three bunnies Karen found abandoned one summer! She has raised them with her own hands, feeding them with an eyedropper. We even took them to Peoria with us and kept them for a year, as Karen didn't think they were ready to be on their own. Those bunnies were like having three small dogs as they ran around our Peoria home. They were potty trained so no worries there. And they loved Karen, following her every-where. We released them back into Superior National Forest (where our cabin is located) the following summer, reintroducing them into the wild.

My first property was not our current Daisy Island but an island called Sunset. I bought it without telling Fuzz. She thought I had lost my mind, and maybe I did. We didn't have a pot to pee in and it was hard enough to make bill payments on my lone salary. But our first visit to the island as a family clinched the deal. However, that maiden voyage, a twenty-minute boat ride to the island, was quite an ordeal for us tinhorns. I didn't know what I was doing.

I was named athletic director the second year at Washington and began working with a great group of guys. One of those individuals was my scorekeeper, Ed Usnik. He, along with a few other men from Washington, was headed north to his old stomping grounds, Eveleth, Minnesota. They asked me if I wanted to tag along. They told me there would be little sleep and lots of fishing. We stayed on Lake Vermilion on an island called Sunset. One of the guys that went on the trip with us, Walt Rocke, had relatives who owned Sunset and wanted to sell it. Walt and his relatives also owned property on Pine Island, a prominent island, 7 mile long that was adjacent to Sunset. The longer we were there, the more I thought about buying Sunset. I had no money and no business sense when it came to buying property, but it sounded like an interesting idea and I pursued it. It might have been nice if I had brought Fuzz into the discussion. Oops!

Lake Vermilion is part of Superior National Forest, an area that bordered, if not encompassed, Sunset and, to a lesser degree, Daisy Island. This area was untouched by development when Fuzz and I first made this move. Initially Fuzz wasn't real keen on owning an island fourteen hours away from where we lived, but she finally came around. Her concern initially had to do with money and the fact that we didn't have any. We had just purchased a house on West Jefferson Street near the high school. I was working extra jobs to make ends meet. I sold New York Life Insurance and, to my surprise, led the division. I did whatever I needed to do to make extra cash to pay for the island and put food on the table. I was lucky that Fuzz was up for a little adventure and that I found two partners, Jack Ekstrum, who owned Jack and Bills Sporting Goods in Peoria, and George Johnston, one of my assistant coaches at Washington, who would help foot the bill. Since the island had three good cabins, we each had our own place along with a boathouse and icehouse. After one summer in Minnesota, the family was hooked. This was after I almost drowned everyone trying to get there.

It was 1959 when Fuzz and I took off on our initial summer adventure, dog, bird (parakeet) and girls in tow. When we arrived at the marina it was overcast, but we went ahead and launched our boat without knowing there was a plug in it. Everything we brought with us, for our three-month stay, was in that boat, included our groceries we had just purchased from the Piggly Wiggly in Virginia. There was no turning back since we had rented our house for the three months we would at the island.

We had pulled Jack Ekstrum's 16-foot outboard motorboat up to the island behind our car. Now that we had launched it, it was filling with water and I didn't know why, until the dock boy said, "Is the plug in the boat?" I said, "What plug?" Then he explained the whole plug in every boat scenario. Everything was wet, including the sacks and boxes of groceries. Fuzz and the girls prayed the boat wouldn't sink. Apparently, we couldn't put the plug in the boat while it was docked and filling with water, so we had to take off and while in full throttle, after the water that had collected ran out, put the plug in. Nothing to it! Fuzz couldn't get the plug in the boat so I had our sixth grader, Gwen, steer the boat while I went to help Fuzz. We survived, docked at the island and then proceeded to unload all of our wet belongings. Needless to say, the trip didn't get off to a great start, and although Fuzz wanted to head home the next day, the long and short of it was that we didn't have a house to go home to; or, at least not for three months. The following day the sun was out and it was beautiful. I was reminded of why I wanted to buy Sunset in the first place, and by noon Fuzz and the girls were in love with the place. We continued our summers at the island and many of our friends visited us there.

It didn't take long for the word to get out about our little oasis. Friends would surprise us as they landed on our doorstep, literally! They would pay someone from the marina to bring them out and they would have their suitcases with them. Since George sold his interest in the island to Jack and me, and since Jack only came for a week or two in the summers, we pretty much had the place to ourselves. With two extra cabins besides our main lodge, we could usually accommodate a family or two dropping in. Most of the time it was just the four of us. It was during one of those unexpected visits from friends that put my boating skills to the test and almost changed our lives forever!

The Wagner's and Alexander's, good friends of ours, brought their families to the island toward the end of the summer. We planned a trip into Trout Lake a much larger lake than Vermillion with much better fishing. The thing was that it was a land locked lake. To get to Trout, we had to portage in. The portage was just across the bay from Sunset, making it very convenient. We took our own small fishing boat and trolling motor along with fishing gear. We had boat cushions that doubled as safety seats in case someone went overboard. They weren't to be counted on in bad weather or extreme events. We did not take life jackets due to space and weight concerns. When we got to the portage, we were trucked into Trout Lake with boat, motor and fishing gear. This would do us for a day of fishing. I knew my way around Trout enough to get us a good mess of Walleye. Trout Lake can be a dangerous lake because of its size and open bays that dwarf most lakes. If a storm strikes, which they often do in Minnesota, boaters are at the mercy of whatever resources they can hobble together. Getting to the nearest land as soon as possible is the best response. The weather looked fine on this particular day, so we made our plans and off we went.

As luck would have it, a storm whipped up quickly at the end of the day. We were just getting ready to head back to the portage for the ride home with our catch. The rain and wind battered our small boat and I was concerned for our safety. I knew we needed to get to shore, any shore, but again, this was a huge lake. With our little motor we would proceed a few yards and then drift a few yards. We were at the mercy of Mother Nature. We began taking on water so I told my friends to throw out anything we didn't need including the fish. Then I directed them to bail out the incoming water. All we had was our boots and a minnow bucket to get this done. I continued to maneuver the boat while they worked to get rid of the water rising in the boat. We weren't making much progress. I had my eye on five small islands called Five Fingers, the last bit of land before we ended up in Big Bay, a body of water aptly named. If we missed the islands, we didn't stand a chance. I was working the bow of the boat toward those islands hoping we could catch the one farthest left in the group, but the wind and waves kept taking us right and we were moving faster sideways than straight. Rain was pelting down on us, and I just prayed we could make that last island. I yelled at the guys and pointed. They got my message.

I kept the front of the boat pushing forward and tried to overcompensate for the wind, but it was virtually impossible to make the boat do what I wanted. We had drifted past all four islands and were just about to pass by the last one when we saw a small ridge of sand and trees jutting out from the bank, so I gunned the motor hoping their was enough sand under water to catch us. Thank goodness the guys had the where withal to jump out and take their chances, as the boat drifted by the island and trees. They were wet but planted themselves firmly in the sand and muck. They grabbed the anchor rope as I jumped out and then we pulled the boat to shore. We were wet, exhausted, but safe. Coaching seemed like a piece of cake to this!

Unfortunately for Fuzz and the other wives, they had to wait until morning to find out if we were okay. We had been reported missing, not having shown up for the last portage truck from Trout to Vermillion. Fuzz knew the dangers of Trout Lake especially in bad weather. We hunkered down and waited until morning. The portage workers were just beginning a search in their big runabout to look for us when we pulled in. It was a great celebration. When we got to the island, the ladies wanted a play-by-play, but we wanted to go to bed. We had been in the rain all night. We had a great story to tell, but the ladies had to wait a little bit to hear it.

NARRATOR:

After Fuzz passed away, Coach and Karen visited Sunset just a few times with the boys. It was time for them to find a place of their own, and since Jack was having health problems, it was decided that Sunset should be sold. After much searching, Coach and Karen found Daisy Island in Daisy Bay. The trip by water was much shorter, just two miles from the marina, about a five-minute boat ride rather than the twenty minutes to

100

Sunset. The cabin was quaint and had lots of windows facing the lake. Karen took to island life quickly and learned how to clean fish, bait a hook and drive the big runabout and fishing boats. Coach and Karen began taking their summers in Minnesota and Karen came to love it. It was a place to get away and relax. The boys found things to do and were more daring in their exploration of the lake than Gwen and Jan had been twenty years earlier. Coach was never really aware of their exploits: jumping off of the high rocks that jutted out over the lake or sleeping on a small rock island overnight, a short boat ride from Sunset. Both sets of kids snuck in their own island experiences over the years (girls in the 50s and 60s and boys in the 80s and early 90s). But God was good, and for the most part, Coach taught his lessons well so that all remained safe. Coach and Karen continue to enjoy their island. The ebb and flow continued.

CHAPTER 8
Moving Across the River

---

*A good teacher is like a candle; it consumes itself
to light the way for others.* Unknown

NARRATOR:

It was 1966 and Coach Van began his first year as an employee of Peoria Manual High School, an inner-city school located on the north side of District 150. Peoria was known as a blue-collar industrial town of over one hundred thousand residents, set on the Illinois River, a "River Town" forty minutes west of Washington. This was Coach's first experience with a school that was comprised of racial and cultural diversity along with income inequality on a large scale. This would also be his first time working in a district comprised of five high schools, along with multiple grade schools and junior high schools, run by a host of bureaucrats. His prior experience was a small-town experience offering only one high school. In these small rural communities, buses were used to transport kids from county areas to the one high school. So the 1966 cultural and political times and the large district, of which he became a part, made for an interesting backdrop to his new experience. The Peoria community, with regard to how blacks were treated, according to a 1940 survey reported in a local Peoria Magazine article, was not much different from the rest of the country. Change was taking place, but not fast enough.

This change for Coach meant he would now be positioned in the midst of a large school district and cultural community driven by politics and he would start his duties during the Civil Rights movement; a movement led nationally by Dr. Martin Luther King Jr. was leading the country in protests for racial equality and on August 28, 1963, he gave his powerful "I Have A Dream" speech on the steps of the U.S. Capitol Building in Washington, D.C. Then, in Birmingham, Alabama on September 15 of that same year, four young African American girls were killed by a bomb while 22 others were injured just for attending the 16 Street Baptist Church. In July of 1964, President Lyndon Johnson would sign the Civil Rights Act into law, preventing employment discrimination. That same summer three college students (one black and two white), working to register blacks to vote, were found dead in Mississippi. In February of 1965, Malcolm X was assassinated, and the following month, a march from Selma to Montgomery took place to protest black voter suppression. On August 11, 1965, race riots broke out across south central Los Angeles, and it took four thousand members of the California National Guard, working until August 16, to quell the violence. The aftermath resulted in thirty-four deaths, and over forty million dollars in property damage, in a forty-six square mile area. Urban communities around the country, including communities the size of Peoria, were impacted. Dr. Martin Luther King Jr. became the conscience of the nation, and he gave voice to many who had no voice, in particular the many black citizens around the country. Sadly on April 4, 1968, in Memphis, Tennessee, two years after Coach began his duties at Manual High School, King would be silenced by an assassin's bullet. But, King's message would live on and the work for equality would continue. Coach began his coaching and teaching duties at Manual in the midst of these events.

COACH VAN:

I walked into Manual that first day of school with much trepidation. I had been happy at Washington. It was a good place to live and work. I thought many times that first year that I had made a serious mistake taking the Manual job. I even had dreams about going back to Washington to my old office, wondering why someone else was sitting at my desk. It was difficult getting used to new surroundings and ways of doing business, especially in a large district with multiple layers of bureaucracy. I had to fill out a requisition form just to get a piece of chalk.

In addition, Fuzz struggled with the move and this hurt me deeply. It was harder on her than I had realized. She slipped into a bit of a depression, and I didn't know how to help her. On top of all this, I was trying to build a basketball program in Peoria, a district that had four high schools and multiple head coaches vying for attention where politics often drove decisions. This was not my style. I found out quickly that basketball was an afterthought at Manual, a less appreciated sport sandwich between the two main sports of football and baseball. Not many Manual students went out for basketball, and very few were taking courses that put them on a college tract. Most students would be heading to work right after high school. Few basketball players had any expectation of playing ball in college.

My first inclination that my job was more political than I first realized came soon enough. I had two ballplayers with the last name Humbles: Henry and Jimmy. Jimmy was Henry's cousin. They would be the first of many Humbles that I would coach over my years at Manual. Jimmy decided not to play football his sophomore year. He didn't discuss this with me before talking to his football coach, Ken Hinrichs. Coach Hinrichs was livid. I wasn't aware of this decision before it was made, but felt Jimmy had every right to make it. He wanted to concentrate on basketball. Ken went to the principal to demand that Jimmy not be able to practice with the basketball team until the football team was ousted from state playoffs. That meant Jimmy wouldn't be in playing shape until maybe mid-December. He would literally miss the first half of the season. Hamm Weldin knew I wasn't happy. He threw it back to us to work out. Ken and I never discussed it further, but without a specific rule, Jimmy was free to do what he wanted. He played and practiced that fall, and over time the situation worked itself out. My thinking was that kids should decide what sport or sports they wanted to play and they should not be penalized for their decisions.

Something else that I was confronted with my first year at Manual was the social and political turmoil in the Peoria community. It was being played out across the nation, and Peoria was not spared. Coming from communities that were all white, I had not really thought about racial disparity. Unfortunately, this was not an area I had dealt with except for the service where the troops were segregated by race. During the war, my mind was on survival; I didn't think about this injustice. When I went to Wesleyan and lived in Eureka, I wasn't confronted with these disparities. Once I began working in small all-white rural communities, I was focused on my job. This is not an excuse for my inattention, just a fact.

Things changed that first year at Manual. I was given a good dose of reality when some of our black and white students went head to head. Most of the time, racial problems arose from outside influences and not within the school walls. I was quickly made aware of social and political realities that come with a diverse urban community. Families on the south side struggled financially as they worked in manufacturing or at the breweries in Peoria. I remembered my own dad coming home after a twelve-hour shift covered in soot. These south-side residents worked long hours for little pay. And even though Peoria was a little ahead of the rest of the nation, having made some advancements with regard to treatment of black citizens and a newly formed NAACP, we still had a long way to go.

At Manual, like every other school, the students were divided into groups or cliques usually based on where they lived. But our students were also divided by race. Our biggest problem in the classroom was cheating, a minor infraction considering. Now, for the first time in my career, I was dealing with racial tensions. The black community, responding to national leaders, was calling for school boycotts, marches and protests. The majority of black kids I dealt with were polite and well mannered, just like their white counter parts. Manual's student population was approximately

20 percent African American, the largest in any Peoria school. It would increase over the years. We were seeing some student unrest with a few fights and altercations early in the mornings before school and sometimes during lunch periods. My daughter was caught in the middle of one of these melees in the school commons area, but a sister of one of my players, Al Jackson, grabbed her and they both took off for a safe place. They had become friends in P.E. class. That was my experience. My players were kids, not black kids or white kids; just kids. But, unfortunately, anytime some kids had time on their hands, something could escalate. It appeared that factions, not always black factions, outside of the school were working to cause trouble inside. At times they were successful. The coaches of all sports teams at Manual were called to the principal's office to see what could be done to quell the disruptions and head off larger altercations. It was decided that coaches would talk to the players to see what they could do as student-leaders. Sports had a great sway within our school, and Mr. Weldin was willing to use anything that could help. Our greatest concern was the safety of the students.

Each coach met and talked with his respective team. After soliciting their help, our student-athletes really stepped up and made a difference. We had an all-school assembly. At the assembly, student athletes—black and white—took to the stage to speak. They talked about the issues confronting Manual and the need to stay in school and get along. They talked about their ability to work together on their respective teams even though they came from different backgrounds and perspectives. These were kids talking to kids. I was impressed at the depth of understanding these kids exhibited and their ability to communicate it. I know that many of my friends back in Washington couldn't understand why I moved to Peoria, and at times that first year, I wondered too. But deep down, I knew it was the right move. It was where I was supposed to be. I was ready for the challenge, and I was ready to grow personally and professionally. My only cause for concern was the difficulty Fuzz was going through.

NARRATOR:

As the 1966–67 season began; Fuzz found herself reading articles in her old scrapbooks, the ones from Armington and Washington. This took her back to a more comfortable time. But she also had fun watching her youngest daughter Jan make friends and enjoy her new school. Jan, a senior, made a smooth transition from Washington to Manual High School. It was a whole new world for the Van Scyoc's, and they were all growing in a unique and wonderful way. With all the activity around the house, Fuzz still found time to start a new scrapbook. Names like Bob Facker, Al Jackson, Mike Anderson, Bob Michael, Duane Demmin and Henry Humbles are sprinkled through the write-ups, which became familiar with time. Sportswriters wrote the play-by-plays and some human-interest stories as Fuzz got to know players and their parents. She began to venture out, and after a year or so, the transition became less difficult. She eventually became a teacher's assistant at Jamison school for students with special needs.

In just a few short years, the Rams grew in numbers adding players such as Willie Williams, Percy Baker, Lee House, Herschel Hannah, Paul Maras, Felix Lobdell, George Caldwell, Mike Davis, Dave Klobucher, Wayne McClain along with many others. They all had stories to tell. Henry Humbles once stood up to a disgruntled teammate who was calling for a team boycott. The boycott never materialized because of Henry's leadership. Percy Baker gave Coach Van credit for getting him a scholarship. As Baker saw it, "I was a nobody and Coach Van worked just as hard to get me a scholarship as he did the best player". During the 1969 Carbondale Holiday Tournament the team had a police escort to their bus because of threats from Carbondale fans. Felix Lobdell, with an impressive physique, stepped in to shield Coach saying, "Just stay close to me Coach!" Players and the community began trusting this new hard-nosed coach. His brand of discipline was not to be messed with, and there were players who rose to his challenge. For Coach, it wasn't about black or white, rich or poor; it was personal. He wanted kids to have a better opportunity than he did, and a good education was the only way to get it.

Coach Van's mission was to get kids to tap into their potential using tenacity and grit. It didn't matter if they were black or white, rich or poor, or if there were other obstacles in their way. If they applied themselves, they could do anything. He was the example. He came from the other side of the tracks, born the sixth child to a family that struggled to make ends meet. He served in a war overseas not knowing if he would have a future, but he kept playing with that little white ball and it took him to college. Now he wanted to see that dream fulfilled in other kids. It mattered to Van Scyoc that kids understood where they came from didn't dictate where they could go in this life. Over time, Coach Van's teams would transition racially from predominately white players to teams of predominately black players as Manual High School's student population changed. Coach Van's coaching style and message remained the same. He saw only the individual. Traits that he believed separated the wheat from the chaff were respect for oneself, respect for others, hard work, perseverance and doing things right. This was what drove Coach Van and what he was trying to pass on.

COACH VAN:

I continued to build my program and hire my own assistants. Two individuals, Virg McElfresh and Chuck Buescher, joined my staff early. Chuck Buescher was a former Bradley Brave, having played for Joe Stowell. After his second season with me, Buescher left for Washington High School. A couple of years later he would land at Bradley University as an assistant. This opened an assistant coaching slot at Manual. A young energetic teacher and volunteer assistant in basketball at Peoria's Roosevelt Junior High School, Ed Brooks had already caught my attention. I spoke to his college coach Guy Richie at Western Illinois University, and he spoke highly of Brooks. The only problem was that Brooks had not played basketball at the college level or had any coaching experience except his volunteer stint at Roosevelt. He was a football and baseball man. I also didn't know if the district would approve his transfer from Roosevelt. He was an African American, and there were no black coaches at the high school level. In fact, I don't know of any black coaches, other than Brooks, at any coaching level at that time. He was young and hadn't been with the district long. By joining my staff, he would be the first black coach hired at the varsity level in any sport at District 150. I had great assistant coaches over the years and was glad when Coach Brooks said yes. Others would join this small fraternity, including Wayne McClain, Ken Meischner, Tim Kenny, Jim Evenhuis, Jerry Stowell and my son-in-law Chuck Westendorf.

COACH BROOKS:

I was at my apartment when Coach Van called. He wanted to stop by. I thought he was coming to talk about kids he was going to get from Roosevelt the following year. But to my surprise, he was coming to ask me to join his staff. Interestingly, I was disillusioned at Peoria. I wanted to coach and teach at the high school level but it didn't appear that I would get that opportunity any time soon, and I was ready to leave the profession. I had talked to my former Manual coaches (football and baseball) to let them know of my interest but nothing had materialized. I volunteered at Roosevelt Junior High School hoping this might open the door to a coaching slot. But again, it looked like my desire to coach had been futile. I felt like Peoria was a dead end; I would be stuck at Roosevelt to maintain discipline, and that was as far as I would go. When Coach Van arrived, he didn't spend much time on small talk. He asked me if I wanted to coach. We talked about my career goals and my desire to be a high school coach. He listened to what I had to say. It didn't take him long to get to the point. Would I consider joining his staff at Manual as a freshman basketball coach? Coach Van knew I had limited experience with basketball but told me I could learn from him.

Coach Van was a very smart guy who considered many different aspects of building a successful program. He never talked about race, but he didn't have to. Instead, he talked about what we could achieve together and how important examples are in teaching and coaching. I could sense that he was aware I might be of some benefit. I don't know what pushback he got from the district office in my hiring, if any, but I moved to Manual for the upcoming year. I didn't know Coach Van very well but had observed his program from a distance. I trusted what he told me. When I took the job, I had no expectations. I was with Coach Van for eighteen years.

I found out very soon that Coach Van was an equal opportunity employer and I was not a figurehead. I was promoted to Coach Van's head assistant my second year over his former Washington player Virg McElfresh. It was a simple decision for Coach. Virg played for him and knew exactly what fundamentals needed to be taught to younger players. Coach Van wanted me to learn as much as I could as quickly as I could. There was no better way for me to learn his system than to be with him at the varsity practices. We all learned that Coach Van made decisions based on what was best for the program, not what was best for any one individual. It worked. The Manual Rams became a team to be reckoned with over the years.

My first year, I watched and listened, picking up as much as I could as fast as I could. One of the first things I did was to tell Coach we needed to recruit a kid named Howard Cole from my PE class. He had more talent than players who were on our squad. Coach agreed with my recommendation. Howard played for us one year and earned all-conference and all-state (honorable mention) recognition—Associated Press All-State Team-Honorable Mention and The Chicago Daily News Mid State 9 All-Conference Team—pretty impressive for one year of competitive ball. Howard wasn't eligible his senior year owing to his age.

It was my second year (1969–70) that my responsibilities with the team changed. We were playing Spalding at home, and right before the pre-game meeting, Wayne McClain approached me. He was one of the players I had coached at Roosevelt. Apparently, Lee House and Dave Klobucher weren't getting along. House told some of his teammates not to pass to Klobucher if they entered the game. Both House and Klobucher were starters on the team. Coach Van never asked me to speak at pre-game meetings, but this particular night he said, "Coach Brooks, you have anything to add?" This was a surprise but it gave me an opportunity to address the situation. I said what needed to be said right in front of Coach. I was straightforward and handled it in a way that I thought Coach would have handled it. I wasn't sure what precipitated this dissention but if it were about black players versus white players, or white players versus black, we needed to end it right then and there. When I was done speaking, Coach Van added that if any players had problems playing on this team, they could hand in their jerseys, and he walked out. They were left with a decision to make. I finished up and then joined Coach Van on the court. We didn't know if any of the kids would take us up on our ultimatum. We found out soon enough as they all joined us and began warming up. We went on to beat Spalding and had no further problems of this kind the rest of the season or future seasons.

From that point on, Coach Van gave me more autonomy and responsibility. I was getting more comfortable in my role, and I immersed myself in his teaching and coaching style. It was a great opportunity and I took full advantage of it. Coach Van was a great teacher without being in your face about it. In his quiet way, he brought me on board. Without any intentionality, we modeled racial respect and cooperation. This isn't to say we saw everything eye to eye, but we had enough respect for each other we could agree to disagree on occasion. Kids and the community saw us working together, respecting each other and having a good time doing something we loved.

Coach and I eventually became running buddies when we were on road trips. During the Pontiac Holiday Tournament one year, we were staying in a "dive" hotel just on the outskirts of town, next to a railroad track. Coach Van called and asked if I wanted to run with him before the game. He said we could run along the railroad tracks. "I'm thinkin' you must be kidding me", I said to him. "You sure you want to do that Coach? People seeing a black man chasing a white man down the tracks or a white man chasing a black man. Either way, it's not good! We had a good laugh and went for our run. Coach Van and I had lots of good times over the years.

NARRATOR:

Jim Bixby was at Manual when Coach Van was hired. As a counselor at the school during Coach Van's tenure, he had great perspective on the man. Bixby said: "Van was adept at taking young talented players and coaches and finding and utilizing their strengths. He could read players and his assistant coaches, pulling out underlying skill sets. Then he would work to enhance it, improve it and make the individual better". During their time at Manual, Coach Van and Coach Brooks were great examples of integrity. "Van had a strength", according to Bixby, "of not caring who got the credit. Brooks was similar in disposition and was always looking at the greater good. They complemented each other nicely. Van exhibited an ability to stay in the background. He did not work to acquire the attention of cameras or the limelight. It was a testament to Van's determination to be successful by making others around him successful". This held true for his staff and for his players.

COACH VAN:

I wanted my ballplayers to be successful as much in life as on the basketball court. In coaching, if I could get kids to do the little things right, it would go a long way in translating to success. And success for us was playing to our strengths as individuals and as a team. If my players improved their individual skill set and minimized mistakes, it made others around them better, and this would equate to success in the game. It wasn't necessarily about what the other team was going to do, but what we were going to do. We had control over that and that alone.

From experience, I saw education as a great equalizer. But it takes hard work. My first year I had a great group of kids and all were hard workers. One of those players was Henry Humbles. Henry was a sophomore my first year at Manual, and when he graduated, there wasn't a lot of interest from colleges. One reason was Henry's size. So I began to make calls to see if I could find a school interested in him. I felt that Oklahoma Central in Ada, Oklahoma, would be a good possibility. From my understanding, a former Manual player had been recruited to play at Ada. However, when I talked to the head coach, he wasn't interested. Seems the previous Manual player quit shortly into the season. Nothing I said could convince him Henry would stick it out. I explained this to Mrs. Humbles and Henry. They were very disappointed. Unbeknownst to me, Mrs. Humbles called the Oklahoma Central Coach and talked to him personally, convincing him that Henry wouldn't quit, even if she had to move to Ada. She told the coach she would even attend classes with Henry, if necessary. Henry got the scholarship. He was so proud when he told me. He was a great kid and was the first of many Humbles who would play for me over the years.

Every Monday through Friday I would wake early, have my coffee and then head down Western Avenue. I would take a right on Aiken Street and proceed down Aiken Hill. I would stop for Mike and Bobby Humbles, and then drive a couple of blocks to Webster Street and within a block or two pick up Wayne McClain. I would drive another two blocks to big Mike Davis' and then onto the Manual High School campus. Over the years, the names of the players I picked up changed and the route changed, but the camaraderie of the players would remain. Harriett Clauson, a teacher at Manual, would provide donuts for the players each morning. She was in charge of our booster club and was known for her unusual hats, enthusiasm and selling treats off a cart, in the hallway, near her classroom door. This was all to benefit the basketball program. We had a large contingency that followed us everywhere we went, even if it meant chartering a bus to attend games. Harriett was a white teacher as were many others. We also had black teachers join our staff over the years. Kathryn Timmes, our guidance counselor, was black. Families and friends who attended our games came from two different races and probably more. The interesting thing was that we all got along. We had a singular purpose—the kids and the game. It brought us together around a shared interest.

The players learned quickly that to play at our level, they had to work before school as well as practice after school. It was this extra effort that often put us a step ahead of our competitors. We would work on dribbling, shooting and footwork before heading off to class. Year after year, I would have a different group that I would pick up or that would just show up before school. I think David Booth gave us the name "Van's Breakfast Club". We would spend a lot of time together, and it paid off. We became like a surrogate family and nothing got in the way of that, including race, ethnicity or economic status. Kids who played for me understood their commitment was to the team and to each other. Anything else was a waste of time, a distraction. The kids also understood my commitment to them. On occasion, players stayed with Fuzz and me. One of those players was George Caldwell. He was with us a week while his dad, a single parent, was in the hospital in Bloomington for a minor surgery. I knew Mr. Caldwell was worried about George staying by himself without supervision. He asked if I would sort of keep an eye on him. Instead, I invited him to stay with Fuzz and me. George Sr. was relieved and George Jr. was nothing but a gentleman and helped around the house. He even brought us a pie at the end of the week when his dad returned.

The first couple of years at Manual were building years with records of 14–10 (1966–67) and then 16–17 (1967–68). Brook's first year, 1968–69, Henry and Jimmy Humbles were seniors and played with Hannah, Jones, Mack, House, Klobucher and Cole. We felt like we were beginning to turn the corner and finished with an 18–8 record. All this was laying the groundwork for our 1972 (25–8) season and fourth place state finish. We would have a young freshman on that team named Bobby Humbles.

I could tell, as a freshman, Bobby was someone special. He was showing great promise, and early in the 1970–71 season, I stuck him into his first game. We were a few points down at Spalding and as the *Journal Star* would report, *"Van Scyoc could have been hung from the rafters for sticking a freshman into a situation like that"*. Bobby was playing against kids much taller than his six-foot frame. But he pulled us out of a hole, and we won the game. During his sophomore year, he got to experience state tourney play. But when he was a junior and senior, we ended with miserable 4–20 and 7–19 season records respectively. Bobby never complained and he didn't quit. His character was on display. He was a class act and could have started for any team in the state. Bobby had something you don't teach—integrity. Many articles were written about him and his deadly shooting. Even though our season records didn't show it, all of our games went right to the wire and were decided by a point or two, all because of Bobby. He was named all-conference and all state, even with our dismal records.

BOBBY HUMBLES:

I was pretty quiet when playing for Coach. I liked to listen and learn. I spent so much time with him that he was like a second father. I remember the first game Coach put me in. I started shooting and I couldn't miss. It was surreal. We won the game, and even though I was really nervous, things felt good. It would be during my junior year that I found myself sitting next to Coach wondering why I had let myself get into that situation in the first place. I was having an off night so I quit shooting and was just handing off to my teammates. It didn't take long before Coach took me out. When I was walking to the bench, trying to get as far away from Coach as I could, he said, "Have a seat" and pointed to the chair right next to him. I thought, *Great*. Then he said, "If you're going to watch the game, you might as well sit here and watch it with me". I couldn't believe it. I was there the rest of the night. Needless to say, I knew I would never make that mistake again. Coach would never take me out of another game for not shooting enough.

I credit Coach for teaching me about the little things that make a person successful in life. I learned not to give up when things don't look good. I learned to give a 110 percent even if the game looks out of reach. I learned that you prepare just as hard when you are climbing out of the valley as you do when you are on top of the mountain, because one of those down days, all you need is a little extra effort to win. I was blessed with many special coaches and great exposure at Manual.

NARRATOR:

From 1966 to 1972, Coach Van worked to build his brand of basketball at Manual. The Rams capitalized on his style of play, and with tenacious defense they were headed to the 1972 super sectional in Peoria. Interestingly, Coach Van's son-in-law, Chuck Westendorf, head coach of Van's former Washington Panthers, would meet Van's Manual Rams in a game billed as a "Family Affair", compliments of the *Peoria Journal Star*. The two teams battled it out for a trip to Champaign and the state playoffs. With the news media writing headlines like *"Does Gwen's heart belong to Daddy",* to build up the family connection, Coach Van was determined not to lose. His two sons-in-law didn't call him the Godfather for nothing. Both of them were very respected coaches in their own right, making this game the Van Scyoc–Westendorf version of all in the family. Sure enough, Manual beat Washington 64–55 in an exciting touch and go affair. Manual went on to take fourth place in the state tournament with players Wayne McClain, Mike Davis, George Caldwell, Wes Gordan, Mike Humbles, Paul Maras, Al Crawford, Bill Jenkins, Bob McDonald, Mike Woods and sophomore Bobby Humbles. Peoria was beginning to sit up and take notice of the south side Manual Rams. After the team's success in 1972, the next three years would see the Rams tested with poor season records even though each game seemed to rest on a last second shot. Only a few points would separate winners from losers. The Rams were never taken for granted.

Fuzz would spend time going to games, and after the games, she along with Coach Van would descend on Hunt's Drive Inn, located just below Bradley's Campus. Fans, friends and players would also show up to talk basketball and either rehash a great win or commiserate a loss. Fuzz continued to add articles to her scrapbooks. The sportswriters would tell of new players such as Bob Darling, Earl Gant, Larry Baker, Frank Welch, Mike Molchin, Bill Taylor, Tim Doolan, Jim Waid, Mike Owens, Tom Bianco and the Stowells (Jim and Jon) who were freshmen. Articles were written about different games and players. Bob Darling's story, told by Bob Leavitt in the *Journal*, had to do with being on time. Coach Van was a stickler for being on time. Just ask any of his former players. According to Darling, he was late just one time. Approaching Coach Van, he explained that he was sorry but he had been in a car accident. Darling laughs now retelling the story as he remembers Coach Van, without missing a beat, looking at him and saying, "You should have left earlier. You need to plan for those things".

COACH VAN:

The Pontiac Holiday Tournament was special in my book and was always something our kids looked forward to. We had lots of success there. The 1975 Chicago New Trier game would be the first and only time we would take home a championship in the 70s. We went on to secure a first place championship in '83, '85, '86, '87, '88, '89, '91 and '94. These championships were against some of the most talented teams in the state including Aurora West ('83), Alton ('85), Chicago's Providence St. Mel ('86), Bloomington ('87), Chicago Oak Park ('88 and '89), Richwoods ('91) and Joilet ('94). Our five consecutive wins ('85–'89) would set a tournament record. We won nine championships in total, a fine achievement for Manual. The tournament organizers always treated us well. We couldn't ask for a better situation. I feel our most memorable games were against Aurora West in '83, Providence St. Mel in '86, Oak Park in '88 and '89 and Joliet in '94.

Our 1975 championship game pitted Manual, a low-income south-side Peoria school, against New Trier, a wealthy well-resourced Chicago suburb, everything needed for a good movie script. The game was touch and go when Mike Moulchin took a charge late in the third quarter securing a 1-point lead for us. That was the turning point, and we went on to win with a 5-point advantage. The sportswriters quoted me as saying, *"Manual was nobody before this win. Now things will be different".* Watching a Manual basketball game was not for the faint of heart. With things looking up, I felt I saw a bright future for the team, Fuzz and me. Little did I know what lay ahead?

NARRATOR:

Shortly after the 1976 season, Fuzz began to have eyesight problems, to the extent that she ended up in the hospital. The doctors had no idea what was causing pressure to build in Fuzz's brain. One thing led to another, and Fuzz and Coach ended up at Mayo Clinic in Minnesota. After months of contemplation, Fuzz was diagnosed with terminal cancer, and they decided to return to Peoria to fight the disease together. School was still in session, and many people stepped in to help Coach Van navigate the difficult task of taking care of Fuzz and meeting his other responsibilities. He wasn't used to taking help from anyone for anything, something he learned from home. It was important to be able to stand on your own two feet; but now he was willing to accept an offer to fly Fuzz home on a private plane, arranged by friends. When they got to the house, other friends had made sure to have a hospital bed on the main floor so Fuzz did not have to climb stairs. And his colleagues at school stepped in to cover classes, pick up kids, check on WECEP and do what needed to be done. The outpouring of love and concern he and Fuzz received humbled him. Coach Van did not leave his beloved Fuzz alone until her passing on October 1, 1976, the first day of basketball practice for the new season.

MIKE MOLCHIN:

Coach Van taught us that game situations always throw you curve balls and it is how you handle those curve balls that count. His coaching life was consumed with using examples and models to get his point across and to teach us how to handle specific game situations. Any good teacher knows this method. But many of us, if we are lucky, may come across a really good life teacher once in our lifetime. These teachers live what they teach. We saw this in Coach Van during the 1976–77 basketball season right after he lost his wife to cancer. We used to go to Coach's house a couple of times a season and she would cook spaghetti for all the players. It was a lot of fun. Now he was coming to the gym, and we knew it had to be hard.

One thing that I remember is that Coach Van set a standard to follow. He wouldn't cut corners and he never asked school counselors for favors on behalf of his players. He believed in natural consequences. When I think back over my career, Coach Van is one person I will never forget during both good and bad times. When we couldn't beat anybody, we really saw what he was made of. He was the same in both highs and lows, and he wouldn't let us hang our heads especially when we played our hardest and still came up short. We were taught to hold our heads high, even in the lean years, and that's not so easy to do. It's great when you are winning and everyone is cheering for you. But it isn't so great when things aren't going your way no matter how hard you try. Coach Van taught us to be "aggressive in our acquisition of knowledge". He had a great work ethic, and he taught that to his players. If you played for Coach three or four years, as far as I am concerned, you were set for life.

COACH VAN:

During the summer of 1976, I had a player Tim Doolan who had signed a letter of intent to go to Bradley University. He had the opportunity to accept offers from other great schools, but he wanted to stay in Peoria and play for Bradley. I was following his situation from Fuzz's hospital room. Bradley University was not living up to its commitment they made to him—the commitment of a college scholarship. According to the new administration, Tim failed to meet Bradley's academic standards by four hundredth of a point. Many former athletes had been allowed to do coursework in the summer to meet this requirement, but not Tim. It all played out in the *Journal Star.*

I met Dick Lien at a restaurant a block from the hospital. He was the Sports Editor for the *Journal Star*. I didn't like leaving Fuzz for even a minute, but I knew Tim needed me to speak on his behalf. Gwen stayed with Fuzz while I was gone. Our meeting and what we discussed was printed in the *Journal Star* on Monday August 9, 1976. The headline read: *"Van Scyoc: Doolan Victim of System"*. Parts of that article follow.

"Dick Van Scyoc had spent the night on a cot in his wife's hospital room, which he has done regularly lately, sleeping in his clothes. The wrinkles had fallen from his shirt but there is nothing double knit can do for the red lines in a man's eyes. Van Scyoc was up early Saturday. There were telephone calls to return, people to meet. One of the players on his Manual High School basketball team was in trouble, and to Van Scyoc nothing except his family is worth more of his time . . . perhaps because his players have so often seemed like family to him. Bradley University, which once announced guard Tim Doolan as one of its basketball recruits, had now said that he did not meet its academic standards for admission. In two telephone calls made Friday from the hospital, Van Scyoc had been told the decision was firm".

"'They're playing with a young man's life'", he said pouring coffee from a pot on a table in a restaurant on Knoxville Avenue near Methodist Medical Center. 'It's too bad, if they think they have to make an example of someone, that it's a boy from a local high school.'

"There was no anger left in Van Scyoc by then, but little understanding either. 'I've given up,' he said. 'That is why I'll talk about it. If I'd wanted to go public, I could have done it before this and made a lot of embarrassing noise. But I don't want to hurt Tim Doolan more than he's already been hurt, which is a lot. I think Tim's been caught in a political thing. I think somebody wanted to show Joe Stowell whose boss. They picked a poor way to do it.'

"Stowell, Bradley's basketball coach, had said if Doolan did not qualify for an athletic scholarship-which he did not, as it turned out, by four-hundredth of a point- he could still be admitted to Bradley under other programs and try to become eligible as a sophomore.

'The boy thinks there was a commitment; the family thinks there was. I think there was, the community thinks there was,' Van Scyoc said. 'This is an almost perfect case of an individual being blasted by the system, the organization, whatever you call it. I respect their right to make a decision. I'm an educator -I understand that the evaluation of a student's potential is subjective. But if there is a problem it should have been resolved long ago. Not like this, not in August.'

"Van Scyoc has coached in Central Illinois high schools for 28 years acquiring a reputation as one of the state's finest fundamental teachers – and much more. His players know Van Scyoc doesn't forget them and in March adjourn to the golf course or to the easy chair.

'He got me a scholarship when I didn't think things like that were possible,' Percy Baker said once. Baker was a reserve on one of Van Scyoc's early Manual teams and played at Grand View Junior College in Iowa. 'I never thought anybody would look out for me like that. He was the new coach. I wasn't any star.'

"Basketball, his family and a little fishing are most of Van Scyoc's life. Bobby Knight, the Indiana University coach, once recruited this area while living in the Van Scyocs' basement in Washington. Bennie Purcell of Murray State boarded there too. 'I talk as much basketball as I can,' Van Scyoc said. But it was to Bradley where many of his best players went. First from Manual, Dave Klobucher, then Mike Davis, Wayne McClain and Bobby Humbles – all but McClain to become starters. 'Go back to Ken Meischner and Ernie Pierantoni from Washington, and I think I've had more players at Bradley than any coach in the state,' he said.

"After the situation with Doolan whose rejection at the 11th hour he finds 'sickening', would he still recommend Bradley?

'Oh, that's difficult to answer right now,' he said. 'I've got friends there . . .' He doesn't want to forget friends, Van Scyoc seems to be saying: even with his innocence lost, but mutual acquaintances seem bent on making him.

"Doolan, only 5-foot-8 and a playmaker instead of soccer, went into the all-star game this summer at Normal almost unknown outside Peoria. On the floor he directed the Class AA North and emerged from the game with a reputation. Van Scyoc saw the all-star game, but was away from Peoria much of April and all of May when his wife Mary, known to him by her childhood nickname Fuzz, underwent tests at the Mayo Clinic in Rochester, Minn. It was then that Doolan got the impression in Peoria that he could go to Bradley. From his wife's room in the hospital late Friday afternoon, Van Scyoc called Bradley to talk one last time about Doolan with Admissions Director Chuck Wharton and Dean Tom Huddleston.

"I was talking to those guys", he recalled Saturday, "and I looked over at Fuzz in bed and she had her fingers crossed. She's sick but she knows what's happening with Timmy and she was hoping. The ball players come up to the house; she gets to know them as well as I do. They're like family, a lot of them".

"Coach Van shook his head. If a man is sad enough, it is a gesture as eloquent as words".

COACH ED BROOKS:

During the start of the 1976–77 season, I was going through my own struggles. I had just gotten divorced. It was shortly after the season started that Van mentioned dinner after practice. He caught me a little off guard knowing he had just lost his wife. He said it wouldn't be much but he would make some sloppy Joes if I would pick up some chips and soda. I told him I was in. That was how we began to spend time together, eating and talking basketball. It was therapeutic for both of us. The two of us began a ritual and it helped us heal. Overtime we went from talking basketball to just talking. I know that even though I had been with Van for a while, this was different. We went from colleagues to friends. When Van met Karen, his second wife, the invites got fewer, but the friendship has lasted and remains strong.

CHAPTER 9
THE MANUAL BROTHERHOOD

Excellence is not a skill; it's an attitude. (Ralph Marston)

COACH VAN:

I remember the principal, Hamm Weldin, calling me into his office right after the school year started in the early 70s. He needed a work-study coordinator for a state-funded program and wanted to know if I was interested. It wouldn't interfere with my basketball practices and some of my responsibilities would change. The teacher/coordinator who had held the job left abruptly. Mr. Weldin told me in confidence that the coordinator had fudged on enrollment in the program (there was no enrollment, no kids recruited for the program) and the budget (supplied by state funds) was in a mess. I was privy to other information about the situation because I would be helping to right the ship, sort of speak, as Manual's program was due for a state audit. I recruited kids from study hall and asked ballplayers to spread the word. I was fortunate that I had some contacts with fast food restaurants because of basketball, so I quickly added worksites. The program gave fourteen and fifteen-year-olds work experience while going to school. They had to keep a certain grade point average to remain in the program, and this was great motivation to do well and stay in school.

I would take some kids to work and then, after their shift, pick them up. Some rode the bus, and some had their own transportation. I was back at school before practice began. Running the WECEP program was much like coaching basketball. It was important for these kids to learn punctuality, consistency in their attendance, giving a good day's work for fair pay, working within a team environment, listening to their boss or supervisor and working out problems in a constructive way. I enjoyed seeing these kids become successful and I was their conduit to learning job skills. I did this until I retired.

MELVIN BURCH-BYNUM (1990–94)

(Active Duty: Major, US Marine Corps):

I was just a freshman when I played basketball for the Rams. I was on the freshman team and I did what I was told to make it to the next level, including lifting weights. This particular afternoon I left the gym and went straight to the weight room. I got right to work lifting, sweating and working my tail off. My goal was to make it to varsity. I was not graced with natural ability, but I was sure I could outwork the other guys on the team. Now in the weight room, I wasn't watching anyone else, just minding my own business. Then I heard Coach. He was pointing at me while talking to the varsity players. "*This* is what hard work looks like. This guy is only a freshman and he is outworking all of you!" Then he looked at me and said, "Good job Melvin". I knew my hard work paid off. That gave me a great boost of confidence. I didn't go on to play varsity ball, but I did continue in the WECEP program. Coach was hard-nosed whether in the gym or classroom. His job was to make you better. I continued to use Coach Van as a mentor and someone I could count on. My mom thought a lot of Coach Van and put him at the top of a list of names she compiled, names of individuals who would give me a recommendation when I need it. I used it when I entered the military. I have visited Coach in his twilight years and wrote him a letter to let him know how he impacted my life. It was good to tell him thank you.

NARRATOR:

The following is a letter from Melvin Burch-Bynum (former WECEP student and freshman basketball player) written to Coach Van. With his permission, it is included. Melvin visited Coach Van in 2016 during Coach's battle with prostate cancer. He followed that visit with this letter.

I will never forget those long rides to Burger King when I was in the W.E.C.E.P. (Work Experience and Career Exploration Program) as well as being on the Manual basketball team. It meant an awful lot to me to thank you for all that you have done for me, from increasing my confidence to my work ethic today. I really enjoyed showing you the list of references (with your name first on the list) that my mother made for me when I signed up for the service. It filled my heart to see you overcome with emotion to know that you made a significant difference in my life. I think it is a beautiful thing when people realize that they have contributed to your success. To see you laugh and then tear up a bit later reminded me of the famous words spoken by legendary college basketball coach Jimmy V in his remarks about fighting cancer where he said. "To me there are three things everyone should do everyday. Number one is laugh. Number two is think – spend some time in thought. Number three; you should have your emotions move you to tears. If you laugh, think and cry, that's a heck of a day". You had one heck of a day on Sunday Coach. In regard to cancer, Jimmy V also said, "Don't give up. Don't ever give up". I say the same thing to you Coach as you battle cancer. I will pray daily that the good Lord continues to keep you in His grip and that you will beat cancer. Regardless of what happens, you have lived a life of purpose and meaning. It is my belief that there are only two occupations that are the most meaningful in life and they are defending/saving lives (i.e. military, police, or doctor) and improving the lives of others through education. Your affiliation with education through sports makes you one of those people I most admire. And learning this weekend that you served our great nation as a soldier in the Army makes you even more admired. You have lived a life of service to others and you have lived a very meaningful life. Thank you for your service, I stand on your shoulders. Again, thank you for all that you have done to help me to be successful.

Sincerely,

Major Melvin-Burch-Bynum

COACH VAN:

It was at the start of the 1976 season that I found myself in a whole different world. Fuzz, my rock in life, was gone. She died the day that basketball season began. After practice I invited Ed Brooks to the house for sloppy Joes and we began to mend, him from a divorce and me from losing Fuzz. It would take time, but Coach Brooks was a great help in that healing process. I used to see him from time to time on the Madison Golf Course in front of my house. This was after he and I were both retired, so he would always have time for a short visit. He has since moved to Arizona. My players were also a great distraction from the pain. I could go to the gym and lose myself in basketball, getting ready for the next game. Working with kids early in the morning until late at night filled my empty days.

I would eventually meet Karen Van Waes while attending a junior high school basketball game at Calvin Coolidge, a school not far from my home. I was there to observe upcoming basketball talent, and Karen's two sons were part of the team. After an introduction, we began seeing each other. It would be a couple of years later that Karen would become my second wife. The boys will tell you it wasn't easy becoming stepsons of a hard-nosed, set-in-his-ways basketball fanatic, and even harder to get used to the Breakfast Club, Manual style. We were in the gym by 6:30 a.m. every morning. I had been in the coaching business about thirty years and my early morning routine was set in stone. Both boys would play for me and would become part of the Breakfast Club. After Manual, they attended Murray State University in Kentucky, the same school Gwen and Jan attended. The basketball community quickly got to know Karen and the boys. Karen started collecting articles and pasting them in scrapbooks, picking up where Fuzz had left off. The four of us weathered the transition and forged a strong bond over time.

In the early 80s, I felt like the Rams turned a corner and made progress, but our teams were still struggling with consistency. Manual would end the 1979–80 season with a 5–21 record, the second worst record in my coaching career. The record was deceiving as many of our losses were by a point or two. From 1981 until 1985, the Rams won/lost records were 23–8, 23–4, 28–2 and 20–4. We had won 90 percent of our games. If we add the 1986–94 seasons, the Rams winning percentage for all thirteen years was 85 percent, or 335 wins to 60 losses. We averaged four losses for each year over that thirteen-year span. This is a testament to the kind of kids we had and their work ethic.

NARRATOR:

Some of the greatest rivalries in Peoria were played at Robertson Memorial Fieldhouse on Bradley's campus, just a short distance from Coach Van's house: Manual-Pekin, Manual-Central, Pekin-Central, Central-Richwoods just to name a few. If large crowds were expected, the high school game location was changed to the Fieldhouse It was tradition and money. The Fieldhouse has since been demolished (2008) to make way for construction of a new student health and athletic facility. Ask anyone who saw a game at the Fieldhouse and they will tell you that the atmosphere has never been duplicated. On cold winter nights, usually Friday or Saturday, approximately eight thousand screaming fans could be found at the Fieldhouse supporting their teams. The quarters were cramped, the bleachers were hard and full, the fans were seated so close to the coaches and teams that often the coaches complained, but they and their players loved every minute of it. The noise level made it difficult for coaches to communicate with players, so Coach Van used large cue cards with coded messages to communicate with his players. Other coaches used hand signals or some other device. It was basketball paradise at its finest, and fans came from all over to be a part of it.

The Fieldhouse was built inside two surplus World War II airplane hangars in 1949 with a unique three-foot raised court. It became the home facility for the Bradley Braves men's basketball program. The facility could accommodate approximately eight thousand fans, when built, but over time was reduced to seven thousand eight hundred. Over the years, coaches complained about the raised floor, the noise and the cramped space between bench and floor. But none of that mattered when the whistle blew and the ball was tipped. Manual and Pekin would battle over the years, often at the Fieldhouse. Manual-Central would play twelve consecutive games there to accommodate the crowds during the 80s and early 90s. Fans never knew, to the bitter end, which team would survive these nail-biting battles.

Central was the cross-city rival that was often a thorn in Manual's side. There was no love lost between these two schools since Central was one of the oldest schools in state and city history. Manual was the ugly stepchild from the south side. But Manual wouldn't stay silent and, over a six-year period, these two teams played to the bitter end with a measly 13 points, over those six years, separating winner from loser.

The 1982 season saw Manual make a run at the state title getting by Central in the sweet 16 and then finishing off Rock Island with a 71–66 win in the first game of the quarterfinals. It would be Mendel Catholic that would surprise Manual with a last second tip in, beating the Rams 53–51 and moving on to state. Fans and players were euphoric one minute, and in total despair the next. But Coach Van had a way of looking for a rainbow when it was pouring outside. His glass was and is always half full, not half empty. This spirit carried him through heartbreaks and spurred him to anticipate tomorrow. He has passed this same spirit on to his players. There was always next year. Manual was on a winning track that would not be matched anytime soon.

COACH VAN:

One of my fondest memories was our win against Pekin in 1984, the game that broke the state attendance record for a regular season matchup. 10,722 crazed fans watched this game. This record still holds. The game was held at the newly built Peoria Civic Center to accommodate the large crowd. It was the hottest ticket in town, and fans lined up at the door three hours before tipoff. It was an exciting and intense game with the lead going back and forth all night. With just a little under two minutes left on the clock and the score tied at 41, Mike Owens hit a two-pointer for us. On our next possession, Frankie Williams was fouled and he converted two free throws, so now we were 4 points ahead with twelve seconds left. We held Pekin in those last twelve seconds to come away with that win. It was an exciting night and things were hopping at Hunts Drive Inn afterword. The final score was 45–41. Pekin would get their revenge the next year and in February would beat us in overtime, 60–59. This was how the battles went.

I had great coachable kids. Some of those who were the most coachable were David and Derek Booth, John Gibson, Ivan Watson, Jamere Jackson, the three Humbles—Mike, Jimmy and Bobby—Jerry Hester, Mike Owens, Wayne McClain, Adrian Hutt, Shettleworth, Syndor, Molchin and Williams. I was fortunate to coach great guards who could direct traffic on the court, guards like Tim Doolan, Lynn Collins, Bobby Darling, Adrian Hutt, Jamere Jackson, Brandon Hughes, Howard Nathan, Morgan, Watson, Coleman and others. I had kids who quit, came back and quit again. Tony Gulley actually moved to Milwaukee to live with his brother, a former Manual basketball player who played for Drake. I think Tony just had some growing up to do. He had a lot to live up to with brothers Al (before I took the job at Manual) and Willie being good ballplayers at Manual. But Tony came into his own, with nothing to be ashamed of, and was a great asset for our team. Val Graham started at Spalding his freshman year but then said he knew he had to come back to Manual. He would tell you that sometimes I needed to take him out of a game just because he got too "streety", playing a little out of control.

My reason for coaching was giving kids an opportunity they wouldn't otherwise have. That was what motivated me. If I could get kids to believe in themselves, I felt I had succeeded and done my job. These kids were good under pressure because they played against pressure every day in practice. They knew our best five players would be on the court in a game. That was where they all wanted to be. Our second team was often as good as our first. The kids we kept would become leaders, kids we could count on. If not, they didn't last very long. If a kid quit and didn't come back, I felt it was better for the team and I told our players as much. If a teammate quit while preparing for a game, they would surely quit in the guts of the game. Everyone had to know his role. When kids practiced hard and played to their strengths, we were a team to be reckoned with.

STAN ADAMS (1978–82):

It was the first day of practice my junior year. Coach called everybody over to the baseline under the basket. He wanted our attention and then told us that each of us had strengths and weaknesses. It was important for each of us to recognize what our own strength was. Not everybody was good at all things. Some of us were shooters; some rebounders and some of us would be better defensively. If we could harness that and play as a team, we'd be hard to stop.

Coach began a story and told us to listen. "We are on a deserted island", he said. "We're stranded on this island and we are tired, thirsty and hungry. We've been here a while and we are getting a little desperate. Where are we going to find food? Then out of nowhere a duck flies by. We have one gun and one bullet in that gun. Someone has to shoot that duck. Who's it going to be?" Coach yelled my name: "Adams, get up here". I hustled out to the floor and he immediately tossed me the ball as he yelled, "Shoot!"

I caught the ball I stepped into my shot, and bingo! It hit nothing but net. Coach yelled, "Duck soup". He kept throwing me the ball and I kept shooting. I was dead on and kept hitting my shots. Coach kept yelling

"Duck Soup". I shot maybe four or five shots and didn't miss once, which was quite amazing with the team sitting there watching me. Right before he dismissed us, Coach said: "Now we know who needs to take the shot!" From then on my teammates called me "Duck Soup".

Coach knew how to get players to play hard and to play to their strengths. Our practices were harder than our games. Coach also inspired camaraderie and a family spirit. He was interested in winning, and to do that, as he would say, "You can't worry about who gets the credit!" He had a way of getting you to believe in yourself and in your teammates. Today, I use this analogy in my job as a store manager. With the responsibility for twenty-five employees, I use this illustration to build a team atmosphere and cohesiveness. When I tell this story, I always think of Coach Van.

NARRATOR:

Manual would on occasion travel out of state to play in high profile invitational basketball tournaments. This was somewhat unusual for most high school basketball teams. During the late 80s and into the early 90s the Rams would travel to the Blue Chip Invitational at the Riverfront Coliseum in Cincinnati, Ohio, twice; the Indianapolis Shootout in Indianapolis, Indiana; the KMOX Shootout in Saint Louis, Missouri; and Pine Bluff, Arkansas. Many of those Manual teams, that were good enough to win it all, didn't make it to the final sixteen or even to the final eight in state play, but they did make a name for themselves and their school. Bob Leavitt, sportswriter for the *Journal Star*, wrote about Manual, leading with the headline: *"Manual takes 133-13 basketball show on the road"*. He painted a picture of a Rams team that had a five-year 133–13 record and was currently ranked eighth in the USA Today high school rankings while heading to Cincinnati. According to Leavitt, the Rams would play in a seven-game tournament that would draw approximately twenty thousand fans each year. The Manual Rams would be playing against Coach Dan Ragland's Moeller Catholic Cincinnati Team. The article explains that apparently the Moeller's coach was David Booth's coach in a Five Star Summer Basketball

133

Camp in Pittsburg, Pennsylvania, the previous summer. According to Booth, Ragland called him stupid during the camp, and now for Booth, beating Ragland's Moeller team would be his ultimate revenge. Manual not only beat Moeller, they blew them out setting a tournament record. The Cincinnati Enquirer headlines identified the Manual Rams as the "best team" in the tournament. Moeller's Coach Ragland would even pay homage stating that "Manual is like a fine wine. They're one of the best teams we've ever played". Leavitt would confirm that *Manual's 94-42 win over Moeller set a new margin of victory surpassing the 21point margin (73-52) set by Chicago King beating Purcell Marian in the tourney's fourth annual event*".

Manual players, who went on to college, became ambassadors for Coach Van's program. They were players who were strong fundamentally. Coach Van's program had great respect, and college scouts would begin to frequent Peoria's south side. According to Coach Van, his kids knew their role on the team and how important it was to play within that role. They were also fundamentally sound and ready to step into any college program and play from day one. These kids had a confidence that set them apart from other players. The *Journal Star* sportswriter Mike Bailey pegged the term *"Manual Mystique"*, in his weeklong 1991 newspaper series on the Mighty Manual Rams. He was the first to put a label on this indefinable quality that Manual players exhibited just walking onto the court. This "mystique" tilted many games in Manual's favor even before the first ball was tipped. Just ask coach Bob Bogle, the second of Coach Van's sons-in-law, married to daughter Jan, about his first experience coaching against the Manual Ram's veteran. This was Bogle's first year as the Pekin Dragon head coach and he would remark after the game that he didn't know if his team would even come out of the locker room the second half. And Bogle wasn't use to losing by large margins either.

This Manual mystique phenomenon would be born out of hard work, sweat, tears and dedication of players dating back to the 1970s and 80s. It would be during the 1990s that it came full circle creating a record of wins that will never be broken. The Illinois High School Athletic Association board of directors changed from a two-class to a four-class state tournament system. The Manual Rams legacy started under Coach Van and continued with his former player-turned Manual Assistant Coach and then Head Manual Coach Wayne McClain. McClain took over in 1994 when Coach Van retired. While still a two-class system, Manual would capture four consecutive first place state tournament championships. Coach Van got the first one in 1994. He retired abruptly, knowing the team would be in very capable hands with his twelve-year assistant Wayne McClain taking over. Upon Coach Van's recommendation, the district named Wayne as the head coach. McClain took the Rams to an unprecedented three consecutive first place championships. It might be said that Van Scyoc and McClain, along with Manual assistants and players, established the Manual Rams as the lone Illinois high school powerhouse in its eighty-nine-year history. This record still holds after 110 years of state tournament play. No other high school basketball team will travel through the same organizational structure and brackets to win four consecutive state titles. Illinois basketball won't ever be quite the same.

The 1981–82 Rams would win 23 games and lose 8. The reserves on this team could have started for almost any team in the state. Brian Watson came off the bench for Manual and they didn't miss a beat. It was always like this, year in and year out, but it was also a precarious place to be, a bench warmer. Watson said it best in a *Journal Star* article: *"You didn't want to cry and have Coach thinkin you're more interested in playing than learning . . . but if you don't say anything, people get the idea you don't want to play bad enough"*.

Each team had a different personality, and this group was no different. Mike Owens, the lone big man at 6'7", was an oddity of sorts being a white guy on a predominately black team. He often found himself explaining unusual situations like when referee Jim Henrickson asked him, during a jump ball, why he wasn't the one in the center jump circle jumping for the tip. "I'm white", Owens remarked not missing a beat. So instead of 6'7"

Owens in the center jump circle, 6'2" Brian Watson was positioned for the toss.

This group had a way of going at each other all in fun. Teammates were always poking fun at Mike, and he fit right in giving back just as much as he got. Reggie and the other guys penned the term "plain old Mike" and it made it into another of Bob Leavitt's *Journal Star* articles. Hopson apparently told Leavitt that "Mike" as a name didn't really fit in with the rest of the team: Reginald (Reggie Hobson), Kennard (Hopson), Valentino (Val Graham), Lewis (Frankie Williams). They all pointed out that the name "Mike" was just too plain. Owens took it all in fun. Leavitt pointed out this comic relief writing about Owens' inability to master the pre-game cadence clapping. Owens was never with the beat. When he became a senior and co-captain, he did away with the clapping cadence, having the last laugh. Reggie Hobson wouldn't let it go though, as he explained in Leavitt's article, *"It's like the scene in the movie 'Silver Streak' when Richard Pryor (interestingly a Peoria Manual grad) was trying to teach Gene Wilder rhythm"*. That was what it was like to teach Mike the cadence. Mike would get his revenge on Hobson. During the Lincoln sectional game, immediately after Hobson scored, the crowd went wild. Hobson thought it was because of his basket. It really was because Mike Owens was entering the game. Hobson realized his mistake, and as Owen's brushed by Hobson, he grinned and said, "What can I say, they love the white kid". (Adapted from a Bob Leavitt's *Journal Star* article).

COACH VAN:

During the 1985 season we had many close games, but one stands out. It was our game against Woodruff. This particular night the Warriors and their new head coach, Ed Brooks, came calling. This was Coach Brooks' first season as a head coach after spending eighteen years by my side. We were squaring off for the first time in a varsity battle and I couldn't have been prouder of Brooks. He had come a long way from volunteering at Roosevelt. That was eighteen years ago and I knew I was a much better person for having known and worked with Coach Brooks. Leavitt coined the matchup as a *"bittersweet win for me and the Rams"*. He went on to call it a *"64-32 baptismal for Brooks' kids"*. Brooks and I spoke after the game and he commented that he knew his kids got an education playing against our defense. He was hoping his kids learned something. I told him Rome wasn't built in a day. He just needed to keep doing what he knew worked.

As the 1984–85 season rolled along, we pulled out some exciting victories. One of those victories was against Richwoods with 0:00 minutes left on the scoreboard. We shot two free throws with the game tied and no time on the clock. It would be the Rams' second victory over the Richwoods Knights, 51–50. In just a few short weeks, Richwoods would return the favor and knock us out of tournament play. We did end up sharing the M-S 10 League Conference Championship with Richwoods that year, and we won an unprecedented eighth MS 10 Championship for Manual. We came away from the season recommitted to making the state playoffs the following year, and with seven returning players who were part of the top thirteen AA players in the regions, we felt we had a good shot. Leavitt would tout our returning players Jamere Jackson, Shun Williams, Fred Lee, Curtis Stuckey, Lynn Collins, Shawn Wright and Glen Washington and the rest of the Manual crew as the best *"two"* teams in the area.

The 1985–86 team was well seasoned and had all the tools to make it to the state tournament and possibly win it all. This was a group that could make some noise, and they would. You had to be lucky as well as good to bring home the big prize. And we had six ranked teams to beat: Richwoods (#12), Lincoln (#7), Rock Island (#9), Rockford Boylan (#8), Chicago Simeon (#1) and Rich Central (#5). A number of our reserves, that year, could have started for any team in the state, but they stuck with us and took their turns off the bench. Even though we didn't make it to the final game, these guys never disappointed. They put together our best record—31–2— of any Manual team up to this point and brought home a third place trophy. I felt bad for the kids, not for myself when we got sidelined. Our only two losses, during the season, came at the hands of Chicago Weber and

Chicago King, pretty hefty competition. Weber would beat us early, during the Galesburg Holiday Tournament, 56–64. King would end our season (70–62) and our chances for the state title. We would come back from that loss and beat Romeoville 75– 57 to take home the third place trophy. This would be the year that we broke another record, our own, with an unprecedented fourth *consecutive* Mid State 10 Conference league title.

NARRATOR:

During the 1986–87 season, the Rams were on a terror, fresh out of the gate. It wouldn't be until tournament time and 30 wins in that Coach Van would be called on to put losing in its proper perspective for his tenacious Rams. Coming off another unbelievable regular season, the Rams ran smack dab into a brick wall called Quincy. The upset ended the Rams' tournament run. Leavitt told it best: *"Manual's title dreams sunk in OT, 61-59"*. But the success of a season cannot be measured by one game. The Rams defeated Central three times, and one of those games was played at Robertson Memorial Fieldhouse in front of 5,340 fans. They also won the Pontiac Holiday Tournament, set another conference championship record and held sway over the some of the best teams in and out of the state. The returning players could only think of one thing: it was time to get back in the saddle and be ready for the upcoming season. But the following 1987–88 season would introduce a new element into the Manual Mystique. A player within the Peoria School District transferred from one local high school to its greatest cross-town rival, Manual, stirring up a world wind, right in mid-season.

TOM WILSON (1987–89):

I lived in the Manual community when I was very young, but when my mother remarried, we moved to another part of the city. My new elementary and junior high school fed into Peoria Central High School. I remained connected with the Manual community through my two uncles who were Manual grads and talked it up every chance they got. They both played sports there. Jamere Jackson and David Booth, Manual ballplayers, were good friends of mine. David and I attended the same church, and even though we didn't live in the same neighborhood, we were pretty tight. I was always intrigued with the idea of attending Manual; but wasn't sure if I should admit it, especially since it was a south side school. Not having lived there for quite some time or been around the community itself, it made me feel a little intimidated. So I didn't pursue the idea of attending. However, I would eventually become the adopted child at Manual, and this would set off a firestorm.

My story is unique and because of my situation, Peoria Public Schools would change their district policy on in-district athletic transfers. An athlete transferring from one in-district school to another in-district school would be subject to this change. Peoria schools are defined by boundaries and each school has some autonomy; however, the district sets certain district policies that all schools must follow. My political nightmare began in 1986 simply because I chose to transfer from Central High School to Manual High School in the middle of my sophomore year. Oh yeah, I guess I should mention that it was in the middle of basketball season and Manual was our biggest city rival.

Right up front, it must be said that no one from Manual recruited me. Coach Van never tried to entice me or even talked to me about coming to Manual. He wouldn't do that no matter who it was. It just wasn't in his DNA. No money changed hands and no bribes were offered for me to transfer. I decided to do this all on my own, and I can't emphasize this enough. My uncles always wanted me at Manual, but that was family.

It was during my freshman year at Central that David and Jamere were returning from Champaign with a third place trophy and a big parade. I, along with a few of my buddies from Central, went to the parade to congratulate them. It was the first time I had been to this kind of celebration. It got back to my coach that we attended, and unfortunately things weren't the same after that. Over time, playing at Central got more difficult and my parents were aware of my struggle. I couldn't find my footing or put my finger on what was happening, but it affected every area of my life. And of course my family, who still had a house in the Manual district, thought we should move to the Manual community.

Everything came to a head during the Manual-Central match-up my sophomore year. As a Central Lion, I didn't get much playing time until late in the game. When I did enter the game, we were losing by quite a bit. I led a rally to get us close to the finish line, but we came up short. When I left the gym after that game, I knew I had played my last game for Central High School. Sportswriters had been speculating that I might transfer, giving credence to the rumors.

High school basketball is a big thing in Peoria. Being a major story in the paper was not my idea of fun. I was scared to death, and I was wondering how this would play out. When I got home, my parents and extended family sat down and talked about the pros and cons of this tough decision. They knew I had been struggling at Central and were concerned. I had confidence that the adults around me would help me sort things out and help me come to a decision that would serve all parties well. I also hoped, first of all, that the adults close to me had my best interest at heart. I definitely didn't want to be treated as a means to an end. I was unaware of the firestorm I was about to unleash! This was a lot of pressure for a fifteen-year old kid given the high-profile nature of the decision and the impact it would have on our community, but the sports media was already speculating. It hit the paper prematurely and, unfortunately, I hadn't talked to Coach Buescher at Central. He was blindsided with the *Journal Star* headline: *"WILSON TRANSFERRING"*. If I have any regrets, it is the way this information came out. It took a couple of days to complete the transfer process through the district. At that point I had established a new address.

As things began to get a little crazy, my uncle called Coach Van telling him we were moving into the Manual district. Monday came and went, and I didn't go to school. The district was getting some blowback, and without a set policy, they wanted to make sure I wasn't living at my old address. The District stationed a car at each one of the two locations they had on file to see if we actually did live at our new address. Finally, I entered Manual High School as a new transfer student. I was apprehensive, wondering if I would like the school and the kids. Manual players were pretty close-knit and full of talent. Would they accept me?

My first day was interesting, because when I walked into the Manual commons, the kids started clapping as Coach McClain met me. He must have been watching for me. All the attention made me a little uncomfortable. When we got to Coach Van's office, it didn't take him long to assess the situation and know I was just plain scared. Things were really turning nasty in the press and around town with people taking sides. Lots of things were being said that weren't true. One of them was that my stepdad accepted a *"bribe"* in the form of a new job to get me to attend Manual. This was not true. When I sat down in front of Coach, I wasn't sure what to say or how to act. I just knew that during that meeting, it was like a weight was lifted off my shoulders. For him, I was a fifteen-year-old who needed some guidance and help in navigating these choppy waters of basketball mania. I had come to the right place.

When it was time for the second Manual-Central matchup I was a Manual Ram. The game was being played at Robertson Memorial Fieldhouse and while I thought things had calmed down, another shot was sent across my bow. I got death threats. The morning of the game, Coach Van came stopped by my parents' house to check on me. It was really early; yet, here he was with coffee and donuts knowing my parents were pretty upset about what was going on. By now, I was part of his Breakfast Club so we were used to Coach Van's early hours. Before school dismissed that day, two Peoria police officers showed up to inform me I wouldn't be going home, based on a credible threat that was made. They had confirmed with my parents that I was to go to my uncle's house and stay there until game time. Manual-Central playing at the Fieldhouse was a big deal. The team was going to meet at Lynn Collin's house. He lived a couple blocks from the Fieldhouse and the team was going to walk there together. I didn't get to join them. I had to sneak in the back door with a small contingent of family. The good news was that I was okay and we won the game. Things got better over time.

I learned much over the few years that I played for Coach Van. I learned that we were not just kids but *his kids*. We weren't a means to an end, a way to bring Coach a little glory or garner him another award. That just wasn't his interest. His interest was outside of himself, and he used every win and loss as a life lesson to make us better human beings. It was his interest in our futures and our success that was evident, and it was evident through the amount of time he spent with us. Time is that one commodity you never get back once it's spent. Coach Van's family missed that time that he was with us making sure we were headed down the right path. And by changing our lives, he changed the lives of those individuals' lives we touched: our wives, our children, our parents, co-workers and friends. Ask anyone who has played for Coach Van. He was not only our high school basketball coach, but he was our surrogate father, protector, teacher, mentor and sometimes our mother. He would laugh with us, cry with us, nudge us, kick us in the pants and yell at us. But every one of his players did not for one second think that Coach Van would not go to the mat for his players.

I have tried to live my life by the principles I learned being part of the Manual Rams basketball team. I am so fortunate to be part of that Manual Brotherhood. I am now a global sourcing manager. It's a great job, and I like to think of myself as successful. At Manual, when I played, there were lots of things kids got caught up in that would ruin their chances for success. Coach worked to keep us away from all that. He carried us through. I still remember his yelling "Wilson!" at the top of his lungs in practice when I missed an easy tip-in from right under the basket.

I was 6'8" and didn't have any excuse for missing easy buckets. One practice when I missed, I saw Coach take off running toward me right after he yelled my name. He looked pretty mad. I honestly didn't know what he was going to do. I was thinking, *Coach is gonna kill me*, so I took off running. By now the whole team and coaches were watching and enjoying every minute. As I ran faster, so did Coach. Now, I ran track so I was pretty fast, but I couldn't shake him. I was thinking; *how's this old dude keeping up with me!* He nearly caught me, but once he got close enough, he slowed down and a smile crossed his face. Thank goodness, the run must have cooled him off. We laugh about it to this day.

NARRATOR:

During the 1986–87 season, the Rams beat the Central Lions twice and then once in state tourney play. The Rams were responsible for three of Central's five losses during their 20–5 season. Beating Central was the boost the Rams needed, as they got ready for Rock Island and the super sectional. The Rams defeated Rock Island for the second time in two years and that put them into a matchup with their nemesis, Quincy. It would be that darn quarterfinal game in tourney play, and a well-oiled Quincy team, that would up-end the Rams, again! Quincy, coming back from a deficit, pushed the Rams into overtime and with two seconds left on the clock, a Quincy player scored from twenty-four-feet. The Rams had little time to regroup. Hopes were dashed in a split second. Manual had been highly favored. The players and fans were stunned. Now Coach Van had to face his kids. What do you say? Coach Van had learned over the course of his life, basketball is a game, a practice for life. Everyone will face defeat in the most difficult of circumstances. He had faced his own dark days when he lost Fuzz. He will be the first to tell you that God will not give you more than you can handle. A lesson hard to learn, but learn we do. This was a game. The kids played hard, executed well and came up short. It was time to shake it off and move on.

COACH VAN:

When you coach as long as I have, you have unexpected wins and losses. You never know what hand you will be dealt. It is just like life and a great way to prepare kids for situations that they are sure to experience. How does anyone handle the tough situations, the defeats, and the really tough times in life? I had a new perspective after losing Fuzz. The game wasn't the only thing or even the most important thing; it never had been. It was about preparation, execution, the enjoyment and, then, the ability to handle the results, whatever they were. If I have a hope, it is that I have served my kids well and passed on these life lessons. I also wanted to pass on the value of education. Basketball was a conduit to college and greater knowledge beyond what one knows only by their circumstance. One of my greatest pleasures was to see Manual players earn college scholarships through their hard work, sacrifice and basketball talent. As the years passed, more and more Rams went off to college. Many accomplished great things at the different colleges they attended. Some of those college players were Jamere Jackson (Notre Dame), Curtis Stuckey, Al Jackson, Wayne McClain, Bobby Humbles, Jerry Fisher Mike Davis, Dave Klobucher (Bradley), Jerry Hester (University of Illinois), Lynn Collins (Arizona State), David Booth and Howard Nathan (De Paul). They all have stories to tell.

Jamere Jackson was one of the strongest academic students that played for me at Manual, and I had some players who were very good students. He was heavily recruited and had lots of opportunities. He was looking toward Wisconsin, until Notre Dame entered the picture. Wisconsin had called the school to find out if Jamere was going to accept their offer. I was on the phone with Notre Dame when Wisconsin called. I had to do a balancing act and we pushed Wisconsin off until Monday for their answer. Jamere was making a trip to Notre Dame over the weekend. When Jamere left for South Bend, Digger Phelps had someone call me and let me know when he boarded his plane, landed safely and was with university personnel. Every time Jamere attended an event, I was notified. This went on throughout his visit. Jamere called me from South Bend just before he boarded his flight home and said that Notre Dame was the school he wanted to attend. He went on to play for the fighting Irish graduating in four years. He was the team co-captain his junior year and captain his senior year. Jamere was a great ambassador for our program, but we had many great ambassadors whether at Notre Dame, Arizona State or Illinois, and I could go on and on. It didn't make a difference what school these players went to; it was important that they went!

JAMERE JACKSON (1982–86):

Coach has taught me so many lessons that are intertwined in my life. I live by these lessons and at times ask myself, "Where did that come from?" I realize it is a *coachism*, one of the many lessons I learned playing for Coach Van. There are so many principles that I have chosen to live my life by that I learned from coach. One of those principles is in judging *commitment* to an organization. We had an overabundance of talent in and around Peoria when I played. We had talent walking the halls of Manual High School that was far better than the talent on the court practicing for the Friday or Saturday night game. Lots of that talent never made its way on to the team. Coach was a strict disciplinarian. He required commitment, punctuality and hard work. Many of the kids who came out for the team and who knew they were darn good ballplayers would end up quitting the team. They just couldn't cut the discipline. Of course, as players we saw these talented kids quit and were thinking; *what is Coach doing? We need these guys!*

But, as time went on, we found out Coach's philosophy. He said he never worried about the kid with great talent who quit. He learned the kid who quit the team, because he couldn't cut the discipline, will be the same kid who can't handle the pressure in the fourth quarter, in the guts of the game. This will be the same kid who won't be a team player and respect his role on the floor. This is the kid who will let his teammates down. I have taken this lesson to heart and applied it in my business life. I am the CFO of a major US company and am responsible for over seven hundred fifty people worldwide. When one of my employees quits, human resource will reach out to me and ask if they should put together an offer to see if we can entice that employee to stay. Coach's lesson is what I fall back on. I realize that this is the person who will quit in the guts of the deal, will fail at preparation and will not work well with his co-workers. He or she will let us down when we need them the most. So, I tell human resources to let that person go. I would rather develop the next person on the team.

I also value the lesson of preparation. I was a helper at a camp that Coach Westendorf and Coach Van had at Saint Thomas. It was on the night that the parents are invited to come and visit. They sit in the stands and watch the skills their kids have learned. Coach Van was stressing shooting to the parents and kids. I was sitting on the sidelines. Coach said to the crowd, "I have my best shooter here". I was thinking to myself, *Oh no.* The next comment coach said was "I am going to have him come out here . . ." Now I was thinking, *I have been sitting here on the floor, I am cold, haven't had time to warm up, get used to the rim.* The split second in which these thoughts were going through my head, Coach continued "And demonstrate". Then he turned to me and said, "Get out here". As I was making my way to the court he said to the parents, "Don't worry about whether it goes in. Just pay attention to the form". I thought to myself, *don't miss.* My head coach grabbed a ball and passed to me. I shot. Swish, right through the rim. He passed another; again right through the hoop. Then he started talking to me, chiding me: "Don't miss", another and another. He kept increasing the pressure on me. He continued to comment as I shot, "Now don't miss". I made six or seven in a row. He then spoke to the crowd again. He spoke about the player who isn't afraid to be under pressure, who will take the shot. I thought about why I was that kind of player. The thing Coach didn't tell the crowd was that he picked me up every day and hour before school. We would go to the gym and he would work with me. It was preparation, something coach believed in strongly. He was as committed to the players as he expected them to be to him and the program. As Coach said, "Practice builds confidence and confidence builds success". I still prep like crazy. My bosses know that I will not let them down whether doing a presentation in front of Wall Street executives or in front of our Board. I will have over-prepared, one of those valuable lessons from Coach Van.

I would like to think I work hard and put the lessons I learned from Coach into practice. I know when Coach was helping me find a college to attend and extend my basketball career, he would not overstate my case. He simply told recruiters they might not be getting the best athlete they could find but I was a good student, coachable and a good kid. I would like to believe that I was smart enough to know that when a good teacher was willing to put in the time to teach me, a kid from the south side of Peoria, I was willing to soak up and learn as much as I could. It paid off. I played basketball at Notre Dame before graduating in four years. I was chosen as the team captain my senior year. I went on to graduate and enter the business world where I put much of what Coach Van shared with me into practice.

COACH VAN:

During the 1987–88 season, we were invited to play at the Blue Chip City Invitational in Cincinnati. I didn't hesitate. When I was in high school, and whether basketball or baseball, the experience of traveling outside of the community taught me something about myself, and often something about my teammates. It was usually a positive experience that fostered camaraderie and team identity. Playing stiffer competition only helped us improve. When Manual got invited to play nationally ranked teams in other state venues, it did nothing but make us better for it. With a five-year record of 133 wins against only 13 loses, we had gained a little notoriety. Ranked eighth by *USA Today*, during the 1988–89 season, it was an honor to be thought of as one of the country's premier high school teams. Now we had caught the attention of Blue Chip City Invitational played in Cincinnati's Riverfront Coliseum. I told Bob Leavitt I hoped we didn't embarrass ourselves. We would be one of the fourteen teams that would be playing in front of approximately twenty thousand fans. Teams were coming from eight states, and we were representing Illinois. I know David Booth was anxious to beat Moeller Catholic, a Cincinnati school, because of Moeller's coach, Coach Ragland. Lynn Collins on the other hand just wanted to see how the Manual coaching staff, including this old head coach, would handle six and a half hours of rap music played on the trip over to Cincinnati. I must say it was an interesting bus ride. The kids were surprised that I knew a lot of the rap songs they played. Joy, my granddaughter who attended Manual, kept me up to speed.

DAVID BOOTH (1984–88):

I didn't see greatness in myself, but Coach Van did. The work ethic that Coach instilled in me helped me become one of the best 32 players in the country my senior year. Family cannot be underestimated here. My mom wanted the best for me, and she pushed all of us to get our grades. I was slacking off, and because of my grades, Mom grounded me. This was at a time when Coach had scheduled a BC (Blue Chip) camp in Renslar, Indiana, to give players exposure to college and pro teams. It could be the difference between a major college scholarship and no scholarship at all. Coach understood the importance of this opportunity for my family and me. Mom was not basketball savvy, but she was a disciplinarian when it came to "the books". I was grounded for six weeks, a whole grading period. I could go to school and play basketball but nothing extra. I told her about the camp, but she held firm. For her, this was just "fun" and the team could get by without me. Of course, Coach knew it was far more than that.

We were scheduled to leave at ten o'clock sharp, and when Coach said ten it was ten. I saw the time pass: eight, eight-thirty then nine. I was getting nervous. At about nine thirty Coach showed up. The players had filled him in. He came in and sat down with Mom. They talked in the kitchen. Coach wasn't in a hurry, but after about fifteen minutes, he emerged and told me to get my stuff. Mom had agreed to let me go. He had explained to Mom the importance of this particular camp. Parents respected Coach, and over the many years he was at Manual, he had built equity in the community and the families and the parents of the kids who played for him.

Coach sacrificed, and his family sacrificed also. He had a great wife who bought into his philosophy and supported his coaching mission. She gave up time with him and allowed him to touch the lives of the young men on the south side of Peoria. Coach Van built a legacy, and Coach McClain continued that legacy. For a period of time in the 80s and 90s, all you had to say was that you played for Peoria Manual and everyone knew exactly what that meant. For us, a poor community, it gave a degree of pride in something bigger than ourselves.

NARRATOR:

Lynn Collins came from a single parent home and a family of ten kids. He was the baby of the family, and this may be where he developed his cocky attitude. This was why he was the "go-to guy" when Manual found itself in trouble. He was known for his shirt hanging out, his unique hair style and his hard-nosed intimidating play for thirty-two minutes; end line to end line. He was the *"intimidator"*, a term coined by Bob Leavitt based on Collins' play-making ability. Lynn would tell Leavitt, "I'd like to think when I am in there all 12 of our guys can have a great night. I don't want to say that all the guys do is look for me in tight situations. But I know that is when I want to have the ball in my hands". As a sophomore, Lynn garnered some well-earned headlines playing in the sectional finals against Lincoln by hitting the game winning shot: *"Manual tops Lincoln for title, sophomore comes of age with the Rams' game-winner"*. Leavitt used a rich historical analogy of Collins' shot with 0:07 seconds left, writing: *"The World will little note nor long remember the two previous times Lynn Collins fired and fell back to the corner. But if his last shot Friday was not heard round the world, it will at least echo through Peoria Sectional history"*. Collins would say that it was the kind of shot that usually got him yelled at, but not this night. Collins had lots of great plays and well-earned wins.

Highlighted in Mike Baileys' article (1991), Lynn Collins went three years as a starter losing only eight games with a winning percentage of 99 percent. In response to a question about what would have happened to him without Manual basketball, Collins, an Arizona State point guard at the time, was prophetic: "Probably some kind of trouble". Collins said he didn't get back home much and believed the south side had changed. Friends ceased to be friends for whatever reason. The one thing that was important to Collins was coming home and not having to cross to the other side of the street when he saw his old Coach. He would rather be able to walk right up to Coach Van, look him straight in the eyes and say, *"I've made it"*. (Adapted from Mike Bailey's article, 1991)

Leavitt described Collins' four years at Manual as *"learning how to work his magic on the basketball court"*. Who could forget the freshman Collins who had the floor sense to drive and pass to Jamere Jackson for a 12-footer *"with just 0:02 left in the Manual-Pekin game giving Manual a one point victory. Forget the running, in your face, 20 footer Collins made at 0:07 as a sophomore for a two point victory over Lincoln in the Peoria Sectional that vaulted Manual to third in the state tournament. Forget Collins' junior season, when he spearheaded Manual to 31 straight victories and the No. 1 ranking in the state polls"*. Leavitt then went on to chronicle Collins as not only a great ballplayer; but also, a very well grounded young man. According to the article, it was Collins's confidence that made him such a threat on the court. *"He makes plays out of mistakes and his teammates become better when he is playing. He will tell you there was one game when he was scared. 'It was that Pekin game at our place my freshman year. I sat on the bench the whole game and then with fifteen seconds left and us behind by one point, Coach puts me in and tells me to penetrate and make something good happen. I wouldn't have been scared if I'd been in the game even for only a couple of minutes. But with fifteen seconds left . . .' Collins quips"* The article goes on, *"Thirteen seconds later, Collins drew a crowd in the middle of the lane and dished off to Jamere Jackson for the game-winning shot. Van will tell you, he wasn't scared, even with Lynn being just a freshman"*.

COACH VAN:

Lynn Collins was one of a number of good supporting cast members for David Booth. All of the 1986–87 players were competitors, but Lynn, being only a sophomore, was going to be a cut above. He already had lots of experience as a freshman, and as a point guard, he could read my mind. He matured his junior and senior years and it was as if he had crawled into my head and camped out. He had great presence of mind and could run the team from the floor. He could post up and was strong with the ball. He was an exceptional playmaker and could read the floor as well as any coach. He could have made some division one school a heck of a point guard, but unfortunately, Lynn didn't take the books as serious as he did basketball. This cost him a scholarship to a four-year university right out of high school. But that didn't stop him from using basketball to get a good education and career. He accepted an invitation to play junior college ball in Odessa, Texas, and would end his career at Arizona State. Lynn would go into social work and have a fine career. He always had time for younger players and was a huge part of our success.

LYNN COLLINS:

I was one of ten kids. My mom was a strong woman and hard worker. She always made sure we had what we needed. I think Mom spoiled me because I was the baby of the family. We lived on Barker Street near Robertson Memorial Fieldhouse on Bradley's campus. When I played at Whittier grade school, Coach Van had Jamere pick me up for practice and work with me. He tutored me, carried me on his shoulders and taught me what I needed to do on the basketball court. I thought I was pretty tough since I had five older brothers and four older sisters. Coach Van would get on me in practice and tell me I needed to stop being a spoiled brat. I would tell him that he needed to treat the other players the way he treated me; it needed to be equal opportunity harassment. I threatened to leave practice multiple times, probably a couple of times a week. Coach told me if I didn't get it together he would call my mom. And there were times he did. She

151

would be on me and tell me to not miss practice. She would say, "You don't want me to have to come down to the gym". Our parents never worried about us when we were with Coach. He took me aside and told me he was just trying to teach me how to be a young man. He wanted the best for me, and he saw lots of potential that could take me anywhere. He didn't want me to end up walking down the street toward him one day and not be able to look him square in the eye. I asked him what he meant, why I wouldn't want to look at him. He said, "There are a lot of guys who have big dreams and great potential, but one wrong decision, a quick lapse in judgment and they end up in jail or in prison. Or maybe they just end up sitting around wasting their life because of drugs". Coach didn't want that to happen to me. I knew then and there whatever choices I made, when I saw Coach, I would be able to walk right up to him and look him in the eye. I wouldn't have to cross the street and not say anything to him.

Coach was like a mentor and a dad all rolled into one. Being without a dad, I felt he filled a void. I was with Coach as much as my own family. He wanted me to be a leader on the court. I felt like I knew what he was thinking, and he knew what I was thinking. I joked with him that I couldn't be bad because he knew if I had a bad thought in my head. He said I would have to make a choice because I wouldn't be able to do what other kids did. I broke my ankle one season. We had the Pontiac Holiday Tourney coming up and Coach asked me if I could swim. Manual had an Olympic size pool and a diving tank. I told him no, I couldn't swim, wondering what in the world he was asking that for. He said, "Well it's time you learn". He asked me if I wanted to play ball again. I was all for that. He would pick me up at five in the morning and we would go to the Manual pool. Coach had the keys and I would swim using a bogie board or float. I would paddle and do laps for an hour and a half to two hours. I did this twice a day, before school and then while the players were practicing. The first game back after rehabbing, I knew my ankle wasn't ready because I couldn't slide side to side on defense. I didn't want to tell Coach but came up with a running defense so I could keep my weight in the middle. It must have been pretty effective because no one was the wiser. I can remember that during another game I was still nursing the ankle and a kid started talking smack to me and it pissed me off. I was getting mad. Coach McClain loved to see me get mad in games because he said it elevated my game; made me a better player. Well, I was elevated and was getting really annoyed when at just about this same time Howard Nathan threw me a great pass that led to a dunk. I went up high and slammed the ball through the hoop. I may have gotten a technical for the shot, but I just remember thinking as I came down on my ankle that it was okay. I was good to go. That dunk was the icing on the cake.

We had the Central game coming up and I really took on the role of team leader. It just fit. I told all the guys to be at my house early before the game. Mom would have something for us to eat and we would walk to the Fieldhouse on Bradley's campus together. It was the sectional finals. I told lots of kids I knew to be there too. They spread the word. When people started showing up, we must have had a couple hundred people or more. I got the team fired up. I said Coach Van raised us to be family and now as family we had some business to take care of. I wanted to go to the state tournament. You only get one time and you have to take advantage of it. We were ready to play and we all walked to the Fieldhouse as a huge big crowd, like army cadets. I'd rattle off something like, "We're the mighty-mighty Rams". Then the crowd and players would repeat it: "We're the mighty-mighty Rams". Coach didn't know where we were and was getting worried. It was quite a sight for him to see this big crowd of people arriving at the Fieldhouse singing this song. We were higher than a kite, and Coach didn't even have to coach much. I told him, "Coach I got this. We are ready to play". We opened the quarter 25–2. We went on to beat Central that night. I just wish we could have gone all the way; it would have been great to do that for Coach.

COACH VAN:

During Jamere Jackson's senior season we went 31–2 and brought home a third place state tournament trophy. One of the reserves on that team was a little-known freshman, Ricky Morgan, who was Jamere's brother. Ricky, who had the same mom and dad as Jamere, also had the same last name Jackson. But Ricky didn't want to be compared to Jamere, so he used his mother's maiden name. It was during the 1988–89 season that Ricky came of age. He was quarterbacking our basketball team as captain while the Rams were setting records with amazing players. Ken Sydnor would score 49 points against Notre Dame, breaking the Mid-state 9 scoring record. Bob Leavitt would report about the *"Manual decade of the 80's"*, our fifth straight Pontiac Tournament title beating Chicago's Oak Park-River Forest, 75–50, highlighting our overall Pontiac tournament record of 32 wins to 5 losses over the decades. This was the year we secured our sixth consecutive Pontiac Tourney championship, a tourney record. Manual's average margin of victory was 22 points. One of my most memorable wins, that year, was when we traveled to Saint Louis and defeated Vashon High School, a premier Missouri powerhouse. We would play and beat Vashon three times, twice at Vashon and once in the Collinsville Invitational Tourney in Collinsville, Illinois.

NARRATOR:

February was an intense month for the Rams. Bob Leavitt would write about the Vashon game touting it as two *"powerhouses butting heads"*. The headline read *"David-Goliath II: Manual cuts down Vashon"*. It was February 11, 1989, when Manual beat *USA Today's* nineteenth nationally ranked Saint Louis' Vashon High School team in a tight game, 42–40. Vashon had front-line players, 6'9", 6'11" and 6'8". Manual's tallest player was 6'2", Ken Syndor. Manual would return to play river city foes with a game against Peoria Central. Central would upend Manual with a win, 54–53, but Manual would regain their footing by defeating Southeast Springfield, Morton and Notre Dame. Now they were ready to butt heads with the crosstown rival, Central for the third time. The Manual-Central contest didn't disappoint, however, Central ousted Manual from tournament play 62–61. Another year ended as a new decade began.

JERRY HESTER (1989–93)

FINANCIAL SERVICES/PUBLIC SPEAKING:

I do public speaking to high school students and I give keynote addresses to corporations and businesses. When speaking, I pull on my background, specifically my early days as a basketball player at Peoria Manual High School. I can remember at the end of my sophomore year I got my first recruiting letter from the Iowa Hawkeyes. I was on cloud nine. This was the first major university that had sent me a letter, a young high school player in his sophomore year! Coach McClain, assistant coach at the time, was the first person I ran into and I couldn't wait to show him my letter. He looked at it, and then told me to look at it again. He pointed out that the letter was signed with a stamp. He told me to rub my finger over the signature at the bottom. I did what he said. Then he said, "It doesn't even smear, does it?" Meaning that it was an electronically generated signature. I was devastated. This letter wasn't what I had thought it was. I lost the enthusiasm I had and headed up the stairs to Coach Van's office in the PE wing of the school. When I walked in he could tell something was wrong. He asked me about it. I told him about the letter and about what Coach McClain said, that the signature was automated. First words out of Coach Van's mouth were, "What are you going to do about it?" He didn't hesitate. I said, "I'm going to work harder". Coach said, "What if you work harder, but you are working on the wrong things?" I hadn't thought about that. Then Coach went further and said, "Jerry, if you get up early and get to school by 6:30 every morning, I will work with you on areas of your game that need improvement. Are you willing to make that kind of commitment?" Not knowing what I was really signing up for, I said sure. I began to show up before school. I would work an hour with Coach and we would especially work on my ball handling. I did that the rest of my sophomore year and into my junior year.

155

The first game we played my junior year was against Chicago King in the Danville Invitational tourney. King was a powerhouse and was a great test for our team's determination and skill. We were coming off a season in which we had won second place in state tourney play. I was in the game, and it was intense. I remember making a steal and then dribbling behind my back, something I could never have done during my sophomore year. It just came naturally, from work and sweat during those early morning workouts with coach. He would have me doing all types of ball handling drills over and over until it came naturally, like the ball was an extension of my body. It paid off.

My junior year I received an overwhelming number of letters from major colleges seeking to recruit me to their school. The one that stands out is the very first letter I got. It was from the University of Illinois and was signed by Lou Henson. The great thing about that letter was that Lou Henson's signature smudged! Yeah, it was authentic.

I now work in the financial services industry and on the side do public speaking. I speak to high schools, corporations and businesses. I tell this story to highlight the power of thought. I cover hard work, and believing in oneself, two things that Coach stressed. These are the two things that are evident in my success. I also talk about the book "The Strangest Secret" and its main concept, "*You* become what you think about". This was a lesson well taught on the Manual Rams' basketball court. We had to think like winners to be winners. Coach let us know that many of our games were won when we walked onto the court. We had that indefinable confidence that was evident by how we carried ourselves, and it came across as soon as we stepped onto the court. We thought we were supposed to win. In close games, our confidence alone was worth a couple of points to ensure a win. This is what I learned and what I try to pass on to my audience. I continue to value every lesson I learned when playing at Manual. I am fortunate for the experience.

CHAPTER 10

The Manual Mystique

Success isn't just about what you accomplish in your life; it's about what you inspire others to accomplish. (Terry Wildemann)

NARRATOR:

The last scrapbook I picked up was from February 13, 1990, to August 14, 1994. Kept lovingly by Karen Van Scyoc, the clippings in this book tell the ending story of Coach Van and the young men who played for him. It's the first and the last couple of articles that put the exclamation point on Coach Van's career and his beloved Manual Rams. Headlines from Mike Bailey's 1991 five-part series recaps the program's impact on the south side of Peoria: *"Coaching is the key, Van Scyoc's formula provides foundation for teams success", "Winning: an all the time thing".* Additionally, above a picture of Coach Van, hand on heart, with the team lined up for the national anthem, Bailey writes, *"Why has good fortune smiled upon the Manual program? Blame it on five players named Talent, Attitude, Tradition, Discipline and Coaching. There is also that intangible sixth man, the Manual Mystique, that defeats some teams before they come out to warm up".* And the finale, *"Basketball: the South Side fix (Pressure on the Rams begins on the way to the gym)".* The in-depth look at the Manual Program was a testament to what Coach Van had built in inner city Peoria, a neighborhood that could lull kids into unsavory choices before they made it to school. This was where he lived and worked for over two and a half decades. He would be the first to tell you he didn't do it on his own, but those individuals who chose to join him, bought into his system.

Over the past forty years, Coach Van had been making daily trips to the gym, first Armington, then Washington and finally Peoria Manual. He never missed a day of practice or a game. This included times when he weathered life changing events; losing Fuzz and when Karen, his second wife, was in the hospital during Manual's state tournament championship. That must be some kind of record. Bob Leavitt and Dick Lien wrote articles about Van reaching career records: *"Rams' Coach Van Scyoc closes in on win No. 500"* (1981–82); *"Manual's Van Scyoc bids for 600th win"* (1985–86); *"Plenty of kids, plenty of teams, plenty of years – Manual Coach Van Scyoc closing in on 700th victory"* (1988–89) and finally Leavitt's article *"757 wins and counting – by 24's"* (March 18,1991). The community and sports-writers were anticipating the biggest prize of all for the unassuming Coach Van: breaking Arthur A. Trout's record as the winningest coach in Illinois state history. This achievement came when Coach Van tied and then broke Arthur Trout's record of 809 wins, finishing with a career 826 while securing the top spot. Trout (Centralia, IL) had held the record since 1951. Coach Van's record would stand until 2009. This would be the year Gene Pingatore won his 827th game, breaking Coach Van's little bit of history. Ping would go on to record 1000 wins, and still counting. Steve Goers, who coached at Rockford Boylan, also surpassed Coach Van's record garnering 881 wins. Coach Van continues as third on the all-time wins list kept by the IHSA.

COACH VAN:

I would be remiss not to mention some special relationships I had while at Manual. I had great friends and colleagues like Kathryn Timmes and Jim Bixby, guidance counselors and great advocates for the program. Kathryn was an intermediary between our program and families. She worked tirelessly on behalf of our players. Jim was also a strong advocate for our program and sold it everywhere he went, especially to colleges. I had great assistants. Coach Brooks was with me for eighteen years and then went on to his own success at Woodruff High School in Peoria. He was instrumental in helping set an example that skin color doesn't matter when it comes to achievement. Brooks and I were focused on results and players' success. Another assistant I owe a thank you to is Coach Wayne McClain, who played for me on the 1972 fourth place state tournament team. Wayne coached with me for twelve years and then stepped in as head coach when I retired. All of my assistants were top-notch and could have been successful head coaches anywhere. They choose to remain with our program and I thank them for their loyalty. The newspaper reporters and radio personalities couldn't have treated me better. I thank all of them for their kindness and professionalism when dealing with our program.

My decision to retire came up rather quickly after our 1994 state championship. By then, looking over my career, I felt it was time to step away. I wanted to give Wayne a chance to see what he could do. I didn't want to leave the cupboard bare. I retired on such short notice it caught everyone by surprise, even me! Karen thought I might have lost my mind. One thing I did know was that the Manual Rams would be in good hands with Wayne as head coach, and I told the principal as much. Wayne was my choice for the job. He had great success, and it gave me no greater pleasure than to watch his teams play. I would also get to watch him as an assistant coach for Bill Self at the University of Illinois. He was a big part of the transition between Self and Bruce Weber when Self resigned to take the Kansas job. Wayne stayed with Weber at Champaign and then accompanied him to Kansas State for a year, but returned to the area becoming head coach at Champaign Central. His son became his top assistant and both contributed to turning the program around. I was deeply saddened to learn of Wayne's untimely death a few years after returning to Champaign. He was such an inspiration to so many young men and women on the south side of Peoria. But his influence didn't stop there. We had some great times on the basketball court together.

NARRATOR:

There was exceptional talent being developed on the south side of Peoria, and college coaches came calling. One of those players being wooed was Howard Nathan, a basketball prodigy. He was connected to the Manual program by way of a legacy; his father Howard Cole was the player Coach Brooks had found in PE class those many years prior during the 1968–69 campaign. Playing competitive ball only one year, Cole racked up some notable achievements. To say basketball was in Nathan's blood would be an understatement.

Like father like son. Howard joined the Rams as a freshman during the 1987–88 season and became part of an elite group, joining the likes of David Booth, Lynn Collins, John Deal, Demetrius Clements, James Shettleworth, Jerry Williams and underclassmen Rick Morgan, Damon Hendricks, Tom Wilson, Ken Syndor and Terry Washington; all would run circles around their competition. Nathan's freshman year the Rams finished 29–5. With personnel changes over the next three years due to graduations, Nathan led the Rams to some impressive finishes—22–7, 28–3—and finally the 1990–91 team finished 31–3 and clinched second in state. Lynn Collins, a senior, made a great role model for the young freshman Nathan. He taught Nathan well.

During the final game of the 1987–88 season, Nathan came of age. The Rams were playing for a third place state finish. This was the game in which Collins broke the state tournament record for assists in a single game. Collins got fifteen assists during the third place game. This achievement did not go unnoticed by Nathan. He listened and learned. Mike Bailey would write that Manual players were weaned on man-to-man defense (Peoria Journal Star) and Nathan was no different. Not only would he become adept at defense, standing only 5'10", he would also be a prolific scorer. In his junior high school career, he scored 49 points for Blaine Sumner. Coach would peg Nathan as the fastest player he ever coached and would recount that Howard never lost a ball without getting it back in the same play. The coaches told their kids to listen to Nathan and do what he said when he was directing traffic on the court. In a *Journal Star* article, Sam Davis said of Nathan, *"Howard tells me where to go and if I get there in time, he will get me the ball"*. Leavitt went on to cleverly embellish Sam's point by writing, *"Time waits for no man; neither does Howard Nathan"*.

It was during the state tournament third place game when this basketball prodigy made the transition from student to teacher. With less than a minute left in the Manual-Rock Island game, Nathan ran the length of the floor for a layup with Booth (a senior) trailing close behind. Rather than take the easy layup, Nathan dished the ball behind his back to Booth and Booth slammed it for the easy dunk. When asked about it later, Nathan simply told Leavitt, "it's Booth's time in the spotlight" and "it's what Collins would have done". Then he smiled, the consummate philosopher.

COACH VAN:

If I could explain the type of player the young Howard Nathan was, I would have to use words like quiet confidence, tenacity, hard worker, competitive and a winning attitude. He was well schooled in our system from watching the Manual teams of the 80s bring their "A" game to the gym. He was a gym rat himself, from an early age. Howard had that kind of confidence that tilted the scale in our favor before the ball was ever tipped. But he was a high school student, headstrong and cocky to say the least. He would have his moments and I'd have mine, and I'd like to think I won. I can remember one instance during practice when Howard got hit in the back of the head with the basketball that had been thrown by Westy (Coach Westendorf). The players were supposed to always know where the ball was. He got hit pretty hard. Out of embarrassment or just the fact that it hurt, Howard walked off the court and sat down. I was watching the situation and I gave Howard all of two seconds to rejoin the team. When he didn't budge, I went to him and said, "Howard, you have ten seconds to get back on the court or there's the door". For a split second my heart was in my mouth. I kept thinking, *what am I going to do if he walks out that door?*

161

I waited to see if I'd won or lost. Howard reluctantly rejoined the practice. I breathed a sigh of relief. We laugh about it now.

Our kids were so competitive we had to institute a five-pass rule for open gym, a time when kids came into the gym and played pick-up games. If not, two players who were especially aggressive would ignore everyone else and play one-on-one. Howard was that kid. He loved to take on anyone and show his dominance. Brandon Hughes, a future Ram, was not one to back down. These two would throw my five-pass rule out the window. One night I called their bluff. I gave them a warning. Surprisingly, Howard said they'd just go up to Central's open gym and make Central a better team. I laughed and told them to go ahead. I knew Coach Buescher wasn't about to let two Manual players waltz into Central's gym and soak up playing time at the expense of his program. They must have thought better of the idea, because they didn't miss a beat when it came time to take the court. Soon Howard was back aggravating anyone he could with his quickness, tenacious defense and dead-on shooting. The competition in our practices was something to behold.

HOWARD NATHAN: (1987–91):

I had heard a lot about Coach Van from my dad, Howard Cole, while growing up. Dad was a heck of a player and could have played at a division one school and maybe even the NBA, if he had played ball before his junior year. Dad never tired of telling me about his old coach, and when I got old enough, he started schooling me on the game. We played in the driveway and down at the local court, just for bragging rights. For a while Dad beat me, but after a while and a little maturity, I started beating him. I was having the time of my life, but my competition (Dad) wasn't as eager to have me show him up on the basketball court. He hated to lose!

As a fourth and fifth grader, I lived to go to the Manual gym and watch players like Tony Gulley and Estelle Russell. I enrolled in any local basketball camp Coach Van was involved with and even won some free-throw shooting contests. I pretty much lived on the local basketball courts and always weaseled my way into high school games. I was good enough to help a team with older guys that were short a player or two. This was my first recollection of playing the game I loved.

When I entered Manual and began playing, I was good enough to start as a freshman. I worked to get better. It wasn't always smooth sailing as Coach and I would develop a father-son love-hate relationship; me being a hard-nosed, cocky, wide-eyed teenager and Coach being the ultimate disciplinarian. I should have been more prepared for the discipline because my dad was also a strong disciplinarian. I had the same love and respect for Coach as I did for my dad. I knew he wanted the best for me, and so did Dad. They both told me that where I was going, my friends wouldn't necessarily be able to go. If I wanted to use my talent and allow it to open avenues of possibilities, I needed to understand that it was for me and me alone. That is hard for a kid to understand.

I was part of a group of ballplayers who took the game seriously and listened (most of the time) to Coach. We prepared in the summers, so we could be good and win in the winters. If this meant going out in the early mornings and running hills so we would be in shape; that was what we did. We also made sure we were at the gym when the doors opened, and didn't leave until they closed.

My parents never worried about me when I was with Coach, whether on a trip or at the gym playing ball. They knew I was in good hands. I would learn Coach Van's lessons well, lessons on hard work, working through tough situations, overcoming disappointment, preparation, and being part of a team. I'd use these lessons when my life dramatically changed as a young adult. I was in a horrific car accident that was not my fault. It put me in a wheelchair and cost me the use of my legs. During this time, as I tried coming to terms with my situation, I used those lessons and the mindset they created to help me overcome obstacles. And of course, my teammates and friends were a big part of my recovery. They wouldn't let me forget the lessons we learned when playing for Coach Van. Their encouragement meant the world to me.

I remember the day Coach Westendorf hit me in the head with the basketball and made me mad. It wasn't that I was hurt as much as my pride was hurt. I was better than that. I was caught off guard when the ball hit me on the head. It hurt a bit. Now I was ticked. I had guys watching. I walked to the chairs and sat down. There came Coach Van. Sure enough he said, "Howard you have ten seconds to get back on that court or there's the door". Now what do I do? For one split second I might have thought about walking out the door, but thank goodness, I didn't make matters worse. I hustled back on to the court. Later Coach Van told me on visits to his house that he was really worried about his next move if I had left the gym. Glad we didn't have to find out what that would have been.

NARRATOR:

Coach Van learned early in his youth that there are no shortcuts in life. Now his ballplayers were learning the same lesson, but this time it was on the basketball court. In Manual's gym it was Van's way or the highway. Many Manual students who were good enough to play wouldn't try out. Others wouldn't make the cut, or would quit. Those who stayed believed they were better people for it, players who have long since hung up their sneakers. The last of the Manual scrapbooks, the ones kept by Karen, now talk about the 1990 campaigns, and the first two articles are about Manual's deep bench and a win against Central. The players knew their roles. Keith Sydnor told Leavitt, "When I play its for my shooting. When I don't, its cause of my defense. My part in practice is being whoever the best shooter is on the next team we play". After a Manual-Central game was played at Robertson Memorial Fieldhouse, Nathan made it clear this was his favorite place to play; one reason was the raised floor. It would be during this game that Nathan would score 25 points while sparking the Manual defensive to a win over the tenth-rated Central club. According to Leavitt, Nathan single-handedly outscored Central's starting lineup. Nathan was known for his entertaining comments like: "I brought the jumper cables and as soon as I started the car, the guys were ready to play!" He would also use his over-the-top descriptions to fire up his great supporting cast. According to sportswriters in the area, the Rams hoped the 1990–91 team would do what the '72 and '87 "editions" could not: bring home the championship. So did Howard Nathan.

COACH VAN:

We had a great group of kids during the '89, '90 and '91 seasons, teams to be reckoned with. Sam Davis came of age as one of our taller players at 6'1", next to 6'3" Clint Ford, the tallest. These guys knew they had to play taller than their actual size and often could out-jump and out-rebound anyone. Positioning was key in rebounding. Different players stepped up in crucial plays to make us winners. We were just so evenly balanced and it showed in the 1991 super sectional game against Central. Tony Freeman came off the bench to make five of five, scoring his only 10 points in the last quarter of the game, just when we needed them. He gave us a real boost with a driving layup off an inbounds pass by Nathan and took some shots that, I must admit, had it been any other game, I would have been hollering. We won the game 66–61, and he was the player to step up at that particular time. This is how it went and it was a testament to the players, their work ethic and understanding their roles.

NARRATOR:

From 1981 through 1994, the Manual Rams racked up 352 wins to 70 losses. This averages out to 5.4 losses per year. With that kind of winning percentage, the expression "dynasty" can be applied to the Manual Program. No basketball team in the history of Central Illinois, not the great Pekin teams of the 1960s, nor the Richwoods and Central Teams of the 1970s, won so much for that length of time. During that period, Manual won seven Mid-State 9 Conference titles, including a league record, five in a row: ten regional championships and seven sectional plaques. This translates to seven appearances in the sweet sixteen and five in the elite eight. From those elite eight appearances, the Rams captured two third-place trophies, one second-place trophy and one first-place championship. This does not include the fourth place win in 1972. Coach Van has the most sweet sixteen appearances at ten, is third in state tournament wins considering all levels of state tournament play, had three consecutive elite eight appearances (1986, '87 and '88) and five appearances in the final four. He is one of only two coaches who have garnered a first, second, third and fourth place win in state tournament play. Jerry Leggitt of Quincy is the other.

During his run-up to becoming Illinois' winningest coach in history, Coach Van had the opportunity to beat his son-in-law Bob Bogle (Pekin Dragons). How sweet! The matchup was slated for January 15, 1994. This was Bogle's first year with the Dragons, and even though it wasn't on Van's radar or anyone else's, it would become his last year at the helm of the Manual Rams. Coach Van was sitting on 808 career wins. The deceased legendary Coach Arthur Trout, from Centralia, the school Bogle had just left, held the title since 1951 with 809 wins. Now, forty-five years later, Coach Van would take on his son-in-law to try to tie Trout's record. And Van's Rams did not hold back beating the Dragons 85–54. It was Coach Van, letting his son-in-law know who was the boss. Bogle couldn't have been happier for his father-in-law, and it made the after-game handshake something special, even in defeat. Bogle would have the distinction of being the first to congratulate the legendary coach. It was Coach Van's forty-sixth season and his 1208th post-game handshake (according to Leavitt), and this one was special. It had always been a family affair. Bogle was an assistant in 1974 under Westendorf, his brother-in-law, when Westendorf was at Washington. Bogle would leave for Nashville, Illinois, and his first head-coaching job in 1975, winning the Class A state Championship there, after just three short years as a head coach. Van would lament to Bogle, that the game just wasn't fair (another reason Van didn't hold back when playing against Bogle's Pekin Dragons)! Bogle would take the Centralia post before moving to Pekin. Westendorf would leave Washington to do a one-year stint in Moline before returning to Peoria. He would become a big part of Coach Van's staff, as an assistant in charge of defense. The two sons-in-law married into a family consumed by the game. Westendorf and Bogle privately referred to Van as "the Godfather", long before Leavitt coined the term, using it in one of his articles.

Van traveled to Collinsville on January 23, a week after beating the Dragons, to finalize the inevitable: breaking Trout's record. This came by way of a 71–64 victory over East Saint Louis Lincoln, in front of two thousand spectators at the Collinsville Shootout. Van became a little emotional when Coach Bob Bone, on behalf of the Collinsville Athletic Department, presented him with a gift, a top-notch fishing pole, to mark the occasion. The Manual Boosters Club presented Van with a gold-plated ring inscribed with "810" and the mounted game ball. Van would respond saying, *"My players are great, my coaches, great, my fans, great. Tonight was more than I ever expected. Thank you to the people of Collinsville"* (Leavitt, *Journal Star*).

COACH VAN:

I had many great teams at Manual, but I never tried to get ahead of myself. With the success Manual had over the years, sportswriters would speculate about my chance at doing the one thing I had not done up until that point; win a state championship. The headlines over the years told that same story. The problem with their assumption was that my ultimate goal, in coaching, was to win a state championship. This was untrue. My focus was not the awards or trophies. I always loved the game and the kids; it was that simple.

Coaching basketball keeps you humble. It's that excitement, and the success and confidence the game can breed in a young man that made it all worthwhile. Teams have to be lucky as well as good to go all the way. All of my Manual teams impressed me with their dedication to hard work, their commitment to the team and their outstanding play. It would be hard to rank them or even choose one over the other. The 1985–86 team went 31–2 and brought home a third place trophy. These kids were willing to stick together, many playing off the bench when they could have started for any team in the state. That speaks volumes about their character: kids like Lee, Washington, Wright, Jones, Lobdell, Stucky, Williams, Russell, Deal, Clements and Williams. Then there were the 1986–87 and 1987–88 teams. We would go 31–1 (1986–87) and 29–5 (1987–88). The 1987–88 team would bring home a third place trophy. It was the 1972-1975 teams that played with grit when their backs were up against the wall. We won 4, 7, and 7 games respectively, over those three years. Players like Bobby Humbles, Bob Darling, Al Crawford, Earl Gant, Mike Molchin, Taylor, Brown and others Those teams never let me down and the 1976 team carried me through some difficult days. All my players earned my respect.

I do have to mention the 1991 team run by Howard Nathan. He and his teammates would end the season with a second-place trophy and Howard would be named Illinois's Mr. Basketball, a pretty impressive honor. But Howard has overcome much in his life and his optimism and determination are infectious. He has stopped by my house many times with his dad. It is always great to see him and talk over old times. He is a great competitor who did not let injuries from a terrible car accident define him. Howard was an exceptional ballplayer even as a freshman. He began his basketball education with the 1987–88 team and learned his lessons well. We fell one game short of the top spot. Mentioning these teams is not to take away from any of the other teams I coached. Each team was talented and unique in its own way, on and off the court. They were a constant source of joy in my life, especially when I lost Fuzz. The 1976–77 team kept me sane. I got quite close to each team and the kids who played for me. I hear from many of them on a regular basis to this day.

CHAPTER 11
The Game

Age is no barrier. It's a limitation you put on your mind. (Jackie-Joyner-Kersee)

NARRATOR:

The path to the state tournament was born through, no less than, the Quincy Blue Devils, a team that Manual's Coach Van was 0-8 against, while at the helm of the Ram's. Coach McClain would tell Van that he now has that monkey off his back with a 58-56 win. It was, as Leavitt coined it, *a nip and tuck kind of game.* Manual had four players in double figures for a balanced attack. Quincy cut the lead to 55-53, but with one-minute left, senior Jimmy Cross would score Manual's last three points in four trips to the foul line.

COACH VAN

It would be the 1993–94 team that would captivate the imagination of the Manual community over the course of the season. We were young, inexperienced and often considered the underdogs, given that name by Bob Leavitt in one of his articles during the state tournament. We were not very big. We had two seniors, Brandon Hughes the team leader and Jimmy Cross who got his share of playing time. We had two talented freshmen: Sergio McClain, 6', and Marcus Griffin, 6'6". As the season progressed,

McClain and Griffin got more playing time with McClain moving into a starting role. Marcus Griffin was used for rebounding help and to give us a defensive edge. Junior, Willie Coleman, knew his way around the basketball court. Other players, Ivan Watson, Darrel Ivory, Jimmy Allen (Juniors), Jeff Walraven, Willie Simmons, Courtland Tubbs and Kahlil Gayton (sophomores), shared on-court duties. This was a young team. They were tasked with playing the toughest schedule I had ever put together. They kept our fans guessing throughout the season!

NARRATOR:

According to Bob Leavitt, *underdogs*, was a fitting description for this team. In his article, *Short Rams live on short shots,* he highlights that *no team with starters averaging only 6 feet has won a Class AA state title.* The *1983 Central Lions came the closest with a 6'2" center.* This year, 1994, Manual had an average starting height *of just a smidgen over 6 feet* and was the smallest Elite Eight entry in state tournament play. Manual's first game would be against Chicago Westinghouse; average size 6'2" and tallest player 6'7".

It was the semi-final Westinghouse game that would make believers out of the Manual Rams. Westinghouse, with their Louisville-bound 6'7" center (Dantzler), battled the Rams to a 61 tie at the end of the third quarter. The Rams, slugging it out through the fourth quarter, found themselves up by one point. It would be Jimmy Cross who would grab the last rebound. He would fire it to freshman Sergio McClain who would toss it to senior Brandon Hughes for Manual's 18th layup and a three point lead with 0:24 seconds to go. Westinghouse's Miller would get two chances to score: one a 26 footer that missed and a shot inside the arc with 0:04. Neither would fall. Leavitt quoted Van Scyoc, "*By golly, we're still getting layups off our regular offense*". Westinghouse tried to get in position for a last shot but lost the ball out of bounds. Willie Coleman and Ivan Watson contributed 16 and 12 points respectively in this important contest. It was a young Marcus Griffin who slowed down Dantzler, and Brandon Hughes held Miller in check. This gave the Manual Rams the confidence they needed. Rockford Boylan was next.

COACH VAN:

The only thing missing at the state tournament was Karen. I hated having to leave knowing she was in the hospital. About two weeks before the tournament, she was diagnosed with Hepatitis A. She was getting treatment and recovering but was still unable to leave the hospital. I spoke with her early Saturday morning and then again later in the day. She had a contingent of friends watching the Westinghouse game with her. Karen was worried about my wardrobe. I told her not to worry that Coach McClain had it covered. He had picked out my usual handkerchief neatly tucked in my coat pocket with matching necktie. I had great assistants around me and they never cease to amaze me: always ready to step in and do what was needed. Now with Karen sick, they picked up additional duties. This was while we were getting ready to take on Rockford Boylan, a school that always brought a huge contingent of fans.

NARRATOR:

It would be Van's youngest granddaughter who would say that all she remembers from this game was the sea of green in the opposing stands. Fans from Rockford Boylan were in mass. The Titans' average height was 6' 2½" with their two tallest players listed at 6'7" and 6'6"; however, Manual worked to handle the Titans. In the second quarter, the closest that Rockford would get to the Rams, was 2 points at the 2:12 mark. Manual continued to control the tempo and pulled away in the third quarter 58-53. Boylan would again make a run and come within 4 points (60-56) at the beginning of the fourth quarter; but Manual would capitalize on a couple of steals and never look back, winning 80-67.

When asked about the win, Van would say, *"I think the key for us today was the way we played defense and picked up key steals. You can go*

up and down the line and everybody that came into the ball game accom-
plished something of a positive nature to help us get to the final game. We
really didn't expect to win by that large of margin; but again, it's these kids
who have worked hard all season and because of it, we have a chance at the
state championship."

COACH:

This would be our game of a lifetime. We weren't nearly as tall as the
Terriers just barely over 6ft to 6'6" and 6'7". We were playing two freshmen, one as a starter. They had already beaten us in December at the SIU
shootout in Carbondale, 79-71 making it our fourth loss of the season.
Now, the kids were looking for a little revenge.

We came out strong and ready for bear. With three minutes left in
the first quarter, we were up 11–6. Watson scored the first two, and then
Coleman scored on a break from Hughes. Ivory scored a short jumper from
the left baseline. Hughes coaxed in a short jumper and then hit another 22'
footer beyond the top of the key for 3. It was at this point that Carbondale
returned fire and scratched back to within one at the 2:12 mark making
the score 11-10. Coleman would then score two and Hughes would stuff
the ball off a fast break. Hudson's 18' jumper off the right wing ended the
quarter with the score 15-12.

During the first four minutes of the second quarter we increased our
margin from three to eight points. After Watson hit a three-point, 21foot
jumper, the Terriers began to make their move. They clawed back ten points
going up by 3 (25-26). It was at the 1:56 mark freshman Sergio McClain
muscled his way inside scoring two, and then added a bonus shot as a result
of being fouled. McClain would add another point but Carbondale's Penn
would answer with his own 2 points, ending the half with Carbondale leading us 28 to 25.

During the half time break we talked to the kids about execution. We
reiterated player roles and talked to the kids about working hard. We told

them that they could sleep in the morning but there was work to done this evening and they had to gut it out. They left the locker room committed to leaving everything on the court. I was wondering if we had said enough as Carbondale got the first four points of the third quarter before Hughes knocked down a three-pointer (28-30). Then McClain fouled Tucker and Hudson hit a three. The score was 28-35 before we knew what hit us. But our freshman, Sergio, fought inside and did a heck of a job; and with Hughes' back-to-back 3's, we had gone up by 1. That was short lived as we traded buckets through the rest of the quarter. We ended the third with Carbondale up by one (45-44).

Carbondale had the possession arrow to start the fourth quarter but Watson got a steal and took a 21-footer for 3 putting Manual up by 2. We then traded buckets until Hughes hit two in a row putting us up 53-49. But Carbondale came right back taking the lead 54-53 when an official time-out was called. When the whistle blew to start play, Watson would again come right out of the gate and score 2 on a 14' jumper. Hudson would return fire and the race was on. This was going to go right down to the wire with each team working for any advantage they could muster. I took a time out with 2:44 to alert our players not to make any dumb fouls and that this would be war for the next two minutes and 44 seconds. I told the kids this was what our hard work prepared us for. No one outworked Manual and this was the time to show it. They had to concentrate and execute.

We regained possession as a result of an offensive foul by the Terriers. Ivan Watson turned this into 2 points on a short baseline jumper, (59-56 Manual). But Green returned fire and we were again up by only 1 (59-58). Carbondale took their second time out. When play resumed, Hughes blocked Rashad Tucker's shot with a minute to play. I took this opportunity to call my third time out. I reminded the players to know where Hudson and Tucker were at all times. I reiterated not to foul; to play smart. The teams returned to the court with 50.7 left and scratched and fought for all of 20 seconds before Manual gained possession on a held ball at 0:31.9. At 25.9 the Terrier's Penn fouled us, but it was a non-shooting foul. This stopped the clock. We inbounded the ball only to have Penn steal it! He dished off to Hudson for a 15' baseline jumper that put Carbondale up by 1 (60-59). Carbondale's Cross-would pick up his 3rd personal foul and 5th team foul as soon as we took possession. We were still not in the bonus. Carbondale called their 3rd time out with a one-point lead and 6.5 seconds on the clock. When the two teams returned to the court, we had the ball. Carbondale's Cross-fouled again: his fourth personal and the teams 6th foul. It seemed their strategy was to keep us from having time to run a set play. But now we were in a bonus situation, and we knew that Carbondale would not foul again and take a chance of putting us on the line. They had a one-point advantage and time was ticking away. That's when Penn made a tactical mistake and with no fouls to give; he did the unthinkable, he fouled. And he didn't foul just anybody, he fouled Brandon Hughes. So, with 4.2 seconds on the clock, Brandon stepped to the line in front of 9,845 screaming fans to sink two bonus shots. They hit nothing but net. Hudson would miss a 40-footer and Green tried a 15-foot desperation shot at the buzzer. Neither found their mark. That is when pandemonium broke out! It was a great win and we loved every minute of it.

Brandon Hughes played some game! He didn't miss a shot the entire second half. He finished with 27 points. The rest of our guys also contributed: Watson 12, Coleman 6, McClain 9, Ivory 4 and Cross 3. I was in disbelief after that game. I know I gave Brandon a hug and when asked by the media about the win, I just told them I was in shock. I never imaged what it would be like to finally finish number one. It seemed like every time Troy Hudson got the ball, he took it inside and scored. It was amazing that we held him to just 20 points, especially considering our size. But Brandon Hughes had an extraordinary game. All of the players stepped up and fought all the way to the end. I couldn't have been more proud of our team.

Coach Bleyer from Carbondale was quoted as saying he was happy for Manual but sad for Carbondale. He thought both teams played well and was not surprised with how physical the game was. He indicated that Carbondale was not real good at chasing people around so they had to play a man defense when they got behind. They tried to mix it up using a zone as well to conserve energy. He mentioned that there were a number of fouls at the end of the game and that we kept Rashad Tucker from getting the ball. We also held Hudson in check according to Bleyer's. His last comment was that it was a great high school game.

BRANDON HUGHES (1991–94):

I was a senior Coach Van's last year ('94). Coach always preached work ethic. I was a starter in football and basketball in high school. I already had college recognition and was on track to get a scholarship. Coach didn't want me to ruin my opportunity to play college ball. He was on all of us, early, when things weren't going really well. We were 10 and 6.

This particular day, Coach walked into practice with probably two hundred letters in hand. We could tell he was irritated. He started throwing letters at us, flinging them one at a time like helicopters. He let us have it: "If you won't go to class and work hard, just get out of here". When he got done, he walked out. We just looked at each other. Then we left. He basically threw us out of practice. Point made!

We came back to win seventeen games straight. He had challenged us that started something in us. We began to challenge ourselves. We wanted to do this for Coach, but we also now wanted it for ourselves. The seniors really stepped it up, and the younger guys followed our lead.

We didn't know that it would end with Coach Van's first state title, but how sweet it was. This ended up being his last year. I remember the parade we had when we came back from Champaign. It is something I will always cherish. I worked Coach's basketball camps from fifth grade on. I think of him as a part of me. We are in each other's lives forever. The things he taught me carry me through each day. Much of it I use in my public speaking. I can still hear

Coach shout, "Feet and shoulders square, elbows in, eye on the target, follow through".

NARRATOR:

The final folder that emerged from all of Coach Van's papers was blue and was marked "State Tournament 1994". It contained practice schedules, statistics from the two final games and a running time sheet with play-by-play of the action. There was a practice plan for the Rams. It was computer generated.

There was a letter from Coach Lou Henson (University of Illinois) included in the folder. He wrote, *"I want to congratulate you and the Rams on winning the Class 'AA' State Championship. It is so obvious that you rank as one of the top coaches in the country. I am thoroughly convinced that no team can win the state title without excellent coaching. It is a great achievement to have led your team to that level of success".*

The media press briefing was included in the folder, along with the answers Coach Van gave to the reporters.

On what he thought about the game: Coach Van: "I'm still in a state of shock. Every time the (Troy) Hudson kid got the ball he took it inside and put it in the basket. He's a great player from a great team. It's a shame one team had to lose a game like this where both teams played so hard right down to the end.

On Brandon Hughes play: "Brandon Hughes stepped up just as he has all season and made those two free throws. It was a gutsy play when he took the ball into the corner. He's been the one who has done it for us all season, and I can't tell you how proud I am of him and the rest of these kids. They had climbed a lot of mountains during the season. We aren't very big but these kids played big tonight".

On getting his first state championship: "I've never allowed myself to get caught in the winning and losing. I like working with the kids. We just try to take them one game at a time. It's how I've approached every game during the time I've been coaching. I've been at it 45 years and I can't think of anything better to do".

In stark contrast to Coach Van's computer generated practice schedule found in the folder marked STATE TOURNAMENT, there was another small notebook found. This small book was similar in size to a stenographer's pad, except the binding was on the side instead of the top. It was made of soft brown leather. The notebook was embossed with gold capital letters that read "TEACHER'S DAILY RECORD BOOK". Above those embossed letters was a faded stamped imprint marked "R.L. Van Scyoc". Coach Van then wrote, in his somewhat legible left-hand penmanship, "Basketball Practice". Finally, the date, again in Van's left-handed scrawl: September 1949. This old notebook is almost seventy years old. The line that is intended for "SCHOOL DISTRICT" or "ROOM" contained the word "BASKETBALL". Coach Van's Signature, "Richard L. Van Scyoc", is on the last line, dedicated for "TEACHER".

The notebook pages are discolored, worn and brittle, but they tell the beginning story of a young Coach Van Scyoc's. It's his first job. History comes alive. Dates, times, practice schedule, plays and player names are included. The early pages are sparse with simple directions.

Thursday October 1, 1949

Practice – 4:00 – 6:00 P.M 120 Min.

4:00 – 4:20 – Discussion

4:20 – 4:50 - Shooting Drill (all shots)

4:50 – 5:05 – Passing Drill

5:05 – 5:20 – Change of Direction

5:20 – 5:30 – Blind Dribble

5:30 – 5:50 Scrimmage

5:50 -6:00 Conditioning Drill

Later pages include team names. From Armington: Charlie Fort, Wendell Nagle, Bob Pratt, Darrell Burt, Wayne Dickerson, Bob Eckhardt, Tom Brandt and Billy Atteberry.

Then from Washington: Adams, Bodmer, Graff, Tully, Morgan, Bareis, Messmer, Sizemore, Thrailkill, Johnson, McConogly, Carmen, Brigam and Blumenshine.

Some pages are empty with only dates and times such as *Friday -Oct. 23, 1953, 4:00 to 5:30 – 90 Min, Saturday Oct 24, 1953, 10:00-11:45 – 105 Min* and (bottom of the page) *2:00-4:30 – 150 Min.* But further into the notebook are practice plans: *1) Zone press defense, 2) zone offense, 3) man-to-man defense with strong defensive rebounding, 4) change of side and weaving defense, 5) offense against man-to-man defense, 6) laps, 7) dismissal.* More names were added from Washington: Cherrie, Wagenback, Dalluge, Faubel, Ruble, Hurst, Pool, Essington, Romani, Van Dyck, Crenshaw. The final date in the notebook on the final page is *Tuesday, Nov. 24, 1953.* A short list of tasks follows: *1. Flag raising, 2. Spotlight 3. Shot Chart.* There is one final entry written by Van. It simply states in capital letters, "BEAT TREMONT".

COACH VAN:

Over the course of my life, I learned to prepare. This might have been solidified as important while in the military. It doesn't make any sense to me that if I'm going to put time into something, I'd not do the best I can. It takes the same amount of time to practice whether lackadaisical or with excellence. I also had a hunger for knowledge and wanted to learn all I could about the game. I would attend any basketball camp I could to listen to college coaches. It was when at Washington that I attended a clinic in Kokomo, Indiana. The head coach from University of Iowa, Bucky O'Conner, was there with his team doctor. He had made it to the NCAA two consecutive years in 1954–55 (finished top five) and 1955–56 (finished top four). He, along with his team doctor, gave a presentation and talked about the benefits of weight lifting. Most coaches didn't believe in this and thought weight lifting would be detrimental to their players. I was intrigued. I had a young player at Washington, Gene Thrailkill, who had some ability but was not well built. He was weak. We began a weight lifting program fashioned after what I had heard, and after a year of lifting, Gene added nine inches to his vertical jump. I say this to highlight the importance of being open and receptive to learning new ways of doing things. When an individual believes they have all the answers and that there is only one way of doing something, the world will pass them by.

I always tried to prepare during practice. But my preparation centered more on having kids practice the same fundamental plays to a fault. In a game, those fundamentals would be natural to what they were required to do. Then, and only then, was it time to prepare for our next opponent. Our kids were fundamentally sound. We prided ourselves in that. I wrote up practice schedules and we followed them. There was no use to write up something if you weren't going to use it. There was no wasted time in our practices. Our kids were all business. We weren't running an intramural program.

NARRATOR:

Along with this old stenographer's pad I found another folder. It was marked Coaching Philosophy. Coach Van's "Early Coaching Philosophy" reiterates his belief in practicing fundamentals of the game. The game for him wasn't against the opponent but rather against oneself and the ability to execute and do the right things right. From his earliest time at Washington, he remained true to his coaching philosophy.

VAN'S COACHING PHILOSOPHY

You have to be strong in your choice of objectives. Winning is a long way down the list of things I'm interested in. It's a by-product of other things. More important is how hard you work at something. Each basketball game is an opportunity for a player to measure himself against his potential. Winning is enjoyable when you really strive to play to that potential. I get no satisfaction out of stumbling and bumbling through a game we win. That is losing. The game is against your potential, not against another team.

R.L. Van Scyoc

COACH VAN:

I am approaching ninety-five years of age. I've spent every day of every school term (nine months each year to be exact) for forty-five years, in a classroom or gym. I have tried to make those days count for something. I never did it to win a state championship, but at the end of my career, a group of Manual players decided it was time. This wasn't my most talented team, but they played the hardest schedule I ever put together. We played Chicago Farragut, Chicago King, St. Louis Vashon (a Missouri powerhouse), Cambridge city, Indiana; West Fork, Arkansas; Barbe, Louisiana; Jefferson Davis, Alabama; E. St. Louis Lincoln (twice), Quincy (they beat us in a double overtime), Springfield Lanphier and our regular conference teams; Pekin, Richwoods, Central, Woodruff, Notre Dame. It paid off. If I could tell my players one last thing, it would be that they gave me a great life! I thank each and every one of them from the bottom of my heart!

EPILOGUE

NARRATOR:

It was a year or so after Coach Van left coaching at Manual High school that I approached him with the idea of becoming an assistant in my classroom, a room of junior high school male students ages 13-15 who had social and emotional challenges. This was a self-contained program and we worked to get kids ready to enter the regular classroom, if possible. I approached dad and posed the question. I had another female assistant but felt the13 young men I taught could benefit from a male role model; a father figure, a coach. We had the numbers to justify the additional staff. He didn't think twice. He joined me at a Pekin junior high school. I shared with him a little bit about the types of behaviors he would encounter. I was a little apprehensive knowing the kind of disciplinarian he was. I knew these kids would test his authority. The first day he joined us, I showed the movie, Walking Across Egypt. It's about a young adolescent boy, who is incorrigible, and an elderly woman who befriends him. I used movies frequently to teach life principles. We had a class motto: Whose behavior can I change? Only my own!

Dad was sitting in the back of the classroom watching the movie along with the rest of the class. One of my students, who could be difficult at times, was talking while the movie was playing. Dad turned to him and told him to be quiet so everyone could hear. This student took one look at dad and said, "F- - - You!" and stormed out into the hall. Dad looked at me but didn't move. Dad was intuitive from all of his years in education and he also was willing to defer to me in this situation. I gave him a nod and we went back to watching the movie. What dad didn't know was this particular student often responded to new and different situations in this manner. He used the hall for a place to go and have some quiet time. He knew I would come out and check on him and help him navigate his return.

What was interesting was that over time, this student, along with all of the students in the class, would begin to seek Coach out for help on assignments, or to talk or play a game. My students had a competition on seeing who could get to school first, so they could be the first one to work with coach. He became close to the boys and they in turn developed a loyalty to him. These kids would study with him; play games with him and would take turns teaching Coach how to use his classroom computer. We had a great time and he had wonderful success in helping many of these students get up the courage to re-enter the regular classroom program.

I was humbled to see my dad continue to make an impact on young men. He allowed fate to place him where he was most needed. That was Coach! And he is still coaching and teaching everyone around him. He is teaching us how to age gracefully, keep smiling when the days are difficult and, count our many friends, players, students and family as blessings to be held close. So, it has been quite a ride Dad!!! Congratulations – We finished the book – Bucket list completed!

As Coach Van and I bring his story to a close, we want to leave you with a final thought. Coach has revisited times and places over his 94+ years to reminisce and say thank you to those who have so profoundly impacted his life. As we both enter our senior years (his a little more senior than mine); and after much discussion in writing his history, we've had a chance to reflect on the important things in life. Life is about relationships, making a difference and working to leave the world; or at least our little part of it, a little bit better than we found it. It is not the hours, minutes or seconds we count; but the hello's, I love you(s), I miss you(s), and the thank you(s) that we cherish. So, we want to say thank you to all who have impacted dad's life and contributed to his story. We leave you with this last poem. We echo its sentiments.

What will Matter

Ready or not, someday it will all come to an end.

There will be no more sunrises, no minutes, hours or days.

All the things you collected, whether treasured or forgotten, will pass to someone else.

Your wealth, fame or temporal power will shrivel to irrelevance.

It will not matter what you owned or what you were owed.

Your grudges, resentments, frustrations and jealousies will finally disappear.

Too, your hopes, ambitions, plans and to-do lists will expire.

The wins and losses that once seemed so important will fade away.

It won't matter where you came from or what side of the tracks you lived on.

It won't matter whether you were beautiful or brilliant.

Even your gender and skin color will be irrelevant.

So, what will matter is not what you bought but what you built, not what you got but what you gave.

What will matter is not your success but your significance.

What will matter is not what you learned but what you taught.

What will matter is every act of integrity, compassion, courage or sacrifice that enrich, empower or encourage others to emulate your example.

What will matter is not your competence but your character.

What will matter is not how many people you knew but how many will feel a lasting loss when you are gone.

What will matter is not your memories, but the memories that live in those who loved you.

What will matter is how long you will be remembered, by whom, and for what.

Living a life that matters doesn't happen by accident.

It's not a matter of circumstance but of choice.

Choose to live a life that matters.

Michael Josephson (Nationally known ethicist and radio commentator)

(www.charactercounts.org)

I have tried to reconstruct events accurately. I have included pictures that may bring back a few memories. In no way did I intentionally leave out a name or try to misrepresent a story. I hope this story; Coach Van's story will bring back a time that will make you smile and maybe laugh a little. We certainly enjoyed the days, months, and years that we worked on this book together. Dad continues to talk and reflect on each of the players he was privileged to coach.

Jan (Van Scyoc) Bogle

In mid September of 2006, seventy former players, family and friends gathered together at Illinois Wesleyan University. They surprised Coach Van Scyoc, at a dinner in his honor, raising over $25,000 to endow a scholarship in his name. How appropriate. The scholarship continues to help students from Eureka, Washington, and Peoria attend Illinois Wesleyan University to further their education. How fitting that Coach will continue to help kids get a college education in perpetuity! All income from this book will be donated to the Coach Van Scyoc Endowed Scholarship fund at Illinois Wesleyan University.

Manual teams and records

1966-67

W-14/L-10

1. Mike Anderson (Senior)

2. Al Jackson

3. Bob Facker

4. Bob Michael

5. Duane Demmin (Junior)

6. Henry Humbles (Sophomore)

1967-68

W-16/L12

1. Duane Demmin (Senior)

2. W. Williams

3. G. Fisher

4. P. Baker

5. D. Smith

6. H. Kilver

7. H. Humbles (Junior)

8. J. Humbles

9. B. Jones

10. H. Hannah

11. D. Maras

12. L. House (Sophomore

13. D. Klobucher

1968-69

W-18/L8

1. H. Humbles (Senior)

2. J. Humbles

3. B. Jones

4. H. Hannah

5. M. Mack

6. L. House (Junior)

7. D. Klobucher

8. H. Cole

9. W. Herrod (Sophomore)

1969-70

W19/L8

1. L. House (Senior)

2. D. Klobucher

3. F. Lobdell

4. W. Herrod (Junior)

5. Hagerty

6. G. Hunter

7. D. Roos

8. S. Hunter

9. P. Maras (Sophomore)

10. G. Caldwell

11. B. McClain

1970-71

W14/L12

1. Tony Hagerty (Senior)

2. Ken Mack (Junior)

3. Mike Adams

4. Wayne McClain

5. Mike Davis

6. George Caldwell

7. Mike Humbles

8. Paul Maras

9. West Gordon (Sophomore)

10. Al Crawford

11. Bob Humbles (Freshman)

1971-72

W25/L8

1. George Caldwell (Senior)

2. Mike Davis

3. Wes Gordan

4. Mike Humbles

5. Wayne McClain

6. Paul Maras

7. Al Crawford (Junior)

8. Bill Jenkins

9. Bob McDonald

10. Doug Moore

11. Mike Woods

12. Bob Humbles (Sophomore)

1972-73

W4/L20

1. Al Crawford (Senior)

2. Doug Moore

3. Bob Humbles (Junior)

4. Craig Zafis

5. Bob Darling (Sophomore)

6. Earl Gant

7. Daryl Kruse

1973-74

W7/L19

1. Bobby Humbles (Senior)

2. Craig Zafis

3. Larry Baker (Junior)

4. Bob Darling

5. Earl Gant

6. Daryl Kruse

7. Frank Welch

8. Mike Molchin (Sophomore)

9. Bill Taylor

1974-75

W7/L17

1. B. Darling (Senior)

2. L. Baker

3. F. Welch

4. B. Taylor (Junior)

5. Molchin

6. Brown

7. T. Doolan

8. O'Connor

9. R. Johnson (Sophomore)

10. J. Stokowski

11. A. Moton

1975-76

W17/L9

1. Molchin (Senior)

2. Johnson (Junior)

3. Taylor

4. Brown

5. Doolan

6. Stokowski

7. Washington (Sophomore)

8. Waid

9. Horton

10. King

11. Owens

12. Bianco

13. Jackson

14. Jim Stowell (Freshman)

15. Jon Stowell

1976-77

W12/L14

1. Rick Johnson (Senior)

2. John Washington (Junior)

3. Jim Waid

4. Charles Webster

5. Tom Bianca

6. Jim Stowell (Sophomore)

7. Jon Stowell

1977-78

W19/L7

1. Tom Bianco (Senior)

2. John Washington

3. Jim Waid

4. Charles Webster

5. Jim Stowell (Junior)

6. Jon Stowell

7. Jim Bjurstrom

8. Claude Rutherford

9. Stan Adams (Freshman)

1978-79

W14/L11

1. Jon Stowell (Senior)

2. Jim Stowell

3. Ron Ingram

4. Eric Cameron

5. Robert Lewis (Junior)

6. Stan Adams (Sophomore)

1979-80

W5/L21

1. Robert Lewis (Senior)

2. Stan Adams (Junior)

3. Warren Grayer

4. Estelle Russell (Sophomore)

5. Brian Sanders

6. Perry Drummond

7. Aaron Kelly

1980-81

W17/L10

1. Stan Adams (Senior)

2. Aaron Kelly (Junior)

3. Estelle Russell

4. Brian Sanders

5. Aaron Mack

6. Fred Hayes

7. John Gibson

8. Al Alexander (Sophomore)

9. Robert Buford

10. Tony Gulley

1981-82

W23/L8

1. John Gibson (Senior)

2. Aaron Kelly

3. Aaron Mack

4. Estelle Russell

5. Brian Sanders

6. Al Alexander (Junior)

7. Brian Gaines

8. Tony Gulley

9. Steve Van Waes

10. Brian Watson

11. Mike Owens (Sophomore)

12. Frank Williams (Sophomore)

1982-83

W23/L4

1. Al Alexander (Senior)

2. Robert Buford

3. Brian Gaines

4. Tony Gulley

5. Steve Van Waes

6. Brian Watson

7. Mike Owens (Junior)

8. Frank Williams

9. Fennard Hopson

10. Darryl Hawkins

11. Doug Hines

12. Dan Van Waes

13. Harold Hayes

14. Val Graham

15. Reggie Hopson

1983-84

W28/L2

1. Frank Williams (Senior)

2. Mike Owens

3. Val Graham

4. Kennard Hopson

5. Reggie Hobson (Junior)

6. Chris Daniels

7. Dennis Green

8. Jon Tidwell

9. Adrian Hutt

10. Jamere Jackson (Sophomore)

11. Fred Lee

12. Shawn Wright

1984-85

W20/L4

1. Chris Daniels (Sophomore)

2. Jon Tidwell

3. Adrian Hutt

1. Jamere Jackson (Junior) 8

2. Fred Lee

3. George Washington

4. Shawn Wright

5. Curtis Stucky (Sophomore)

6.   Shun Williams

7.   David Booth (Freshman)

8.   David Collins

9.   James Shettleworth

1985-86

W31/L2

1.   Jamere Jackson (Senior)

2.   Fred Lee

3.   Glen Washington

4.   Shawn Wright

5.   Sidney Jones (Junior)

6.   Tony Lobdell

7.   Curtis Stucky

8.   Shun Williams

9.   Darin Russell

10. David Booth (Sophomore)

11. Lynn Collins

12. John Deal

13. Demetrius Clements

14. Jerry Williams

15. Monty Walker

16. Damon Hendricks (Freshman)

17. Ricky Morgan

1986-87

W31/L1

1. Curtis Stuckey (Senior)

2. Shun Williams

3. David Booth (Junior)

4. Lynn Collins

5. John Deal

6. Demetrious Clements

7. Jerry Williams

8. James Shettleworth

9. Ricky Morgan (Sophomore)

10. Damon Hendricks

11. Tom Wilson

12. Ken Syndor

1987-88

W29/L5

1. David Booth (Senior)

2. Lynn Collins

3. John Deal

4. Demetrius Clements

5. James Shettleworth

6. Jerry Williams

7. Rick Morgan (Junior)

8. Damon Hendricks

9. Tom Wilson

10. Ken Syndor

11. Terry Washington (Sophomore)

12. Nathan Howard (Freshman)

1988-89

W22/L7

1. Rick Morgan (Senior)

2. Damon Hendricks

3. Tom Wilson

4. Kenneth Syndor

5. Howard Nathan (Sophomore)

6. Mike Grayer

7. Sam Davis

8. Derek Booth

9. Lee Reddick

10. Clint Ford

1989-90

W28/L3

1. Howard Nathan (Junior)

2. Michael Grayer

3. Sam Davis

4. Derek Booth

5. Lee Reddick

6. Peter Williams

7. Tony Freeman

8. Kevin Deal

9. Clint Ford

10. Keith Syndor

11. Keith Johnson

12. Jerry Hester

1990-91

W31/L3

1. Howard Nathan (Senior)

2. Michael Grayer

3. Sam Davis

4. Derek Booth

5. Lee Reddick

6. Tony Freeman

7. Kevin Deal (Junior)

8. Clint Ford

9. Keith Johnson

10. Jerry Hester

11. Earl Jackson

12. Brandon Allen

13. Jimmy Cross

14. Brandon Whitaker

15. Shawn Foote

16. Chris Baker

17. Joe Bell

1991-92

W19/L9

1. Kevin Deal (Senior)

2. Clint Ford

3. Keith Johnson

4. Jerry Hester (Junior)

5. Earl Jackson

6. Tom Hayes

7. Adrian Sargent

8. Brandon Hughes (Sophomore)

9. Jimmy Cross

10. Brandon Allen

11. Calvin Powell (Freshman)

1992-93

W23/L6

1. Jerry Hester (Senior)

2. Earl Jackson

3. Adrian Sargent

4. Brandon Hughes (Junior)

5. Jimmy Cross

6. Courtland Tubbs

7. Shawn Williams

8. Willie Coleman (Sophomore)

9. Dan Duncan

10. Darrell Ivory

11. Dwayne Johnson

12. Corey Lloyd

13. Charles Nathan

14. Calvin Powell

15. Jeff Walraven

16. Ivan Watson

1993-94

W27/L6

1. Brandon Hughes (Senior)

2. Willie Coleman (Junior)

3. Ivan Watson (Junior)

4. Darrel Ivory

5. Allen

6. Jimmy Cross

7. Jeff Walraven (Sophomore)

8. Willie Simmons

9. Courtlan Tubbs

10. Kahlil Gayton

11. Sergio McClain (Freshman)

12. Marcus Griffin